Assignments in
Leisure and Tourism
for GNVQ   Book 2

John Ward

The Travel and Tourism Programme

Stanley Thornes (Publishers) Ltd

Published in 1993 by:
Stanley Thornes (Publishers) Ltd
Ellenborough House
Wellington Street
CHELTENHAM GL50 1YD
England

Reprinted 1994 (twice)

A catalogue record for this book is available from The British Library.

ISBN 0 7487 1669 6

Typeset by Stanley Thornes (Publishers) Ltd
Printed and bound in Great Britain at The Bath Press, Avon

Contents

Introduction   v

GNVQ Leisure and Tourism: Summary of mandatory units   x

Acknowledgments   xi

Unit 5: Planning for an event or function
5.1   Planning a festival: Commonwealth Day   1
5.2   Organising a national festival   4
5.3   Government funding for sport in the community   5
5.4   Planning a public meeting about a leisure development   7
5.5   Planning activity holidays   9
5.6   Renovating a children's playground: resource requirements   12
5.7   Planning a conference – the need for a schedule   14
5.8   Hiring premises   17
5.9   Planning schedules   18
5.10 Fireworks at AltonTowers   20

Unit 6: Maintaining information services
6.1   Office technology and information handling   25
6.2   Information and hotel management   27
6.3   Management information systems in leisure attractions   29
6.4   Restaurant management – documentation   31
6.5   Computer applications in the leisure industry   35
6.6   Computerised reservations systems   38
6.7   Using research data for planning purposes   41
6.8   Data protection   46

Unit 7: Working in teams
7.1   Organisation and management at Beaulieu   49
7.2   Teamwork and motivation   52
7.3   Leadership   54
7.4   Conflict and co-operation at work   57
7.5   Games as teamwork training   59
7.6   Quality circles   62
7.7   Teamwork and presenting a good case   65
7.8   Staff appraisal   68

Unit 8: Evaluating the performance of facilities
8.1   Beaulieu: organisational objectives   71
8.2   Visitor attractions – a national code of practice   73
8.3   Company quality assessment schemes   75
8.4   A new airport – the environmental impact   77

8.5   Evaluating the work of a museum – performance targets   **81**

8.6   Evaluating the financial performance of a guest house   **84**

8.7   Evaluating the business performance of a leisure park   **89**

Introduction

General

This book of assignments has been prepared primarily with the new General National Vocational Qualification (GNVQ) in mind, though many of the assignments should prove equally useful to students of other leisure and tourism courses.

One of the main purposes of GNVQs is to provide a national scheme of vocational qualifications which can stand alongside traditional academic qualifications and offer an attractive but rigorous alternative. They are intended to offer a broad-based approach, avoiding a concentration on very narrow vocational skills, which will better equip students either for entry into employment or progression into higher education. Consequently, assignments set on such courses need to be both enjoyable and demanding.

GNVQs are assessed largely on the basis of evidence collected during the course. These assignments are intended to generate a range of outcomes in a variety of forms. Some require student participation in discussion, role play and oral presentation; others demand a variety of written outcomes, including reports, letters, memoranda, diagrams and computer-generated information.

Many of the assignments are structured so that there are some tasks which can be done immediately, these being entirely based on the stimulus material which precedes them. Subsequent tasks will often require discussion and research and are likely to involve co-operative work. The tasks have been designed to generate the kind of evidence required for the cumulative assessment which is central to GNVQ courses

Level of difficulty

GNVQs are aimed primarily at the 16–19 age group, but the long-term aim is to make them more widely available. Most students are likely to be on full-time school or college courses, in some cases combining GNVQs with GCSE and A or AS level courses.

GNVQs are being developed at four levels of difficulty, with Intermediate and Advanced levels likely to be in most demand in schools and colleges. Achieving a GNVQ at Intermediate level is intended to be the equivalent of taking four GCSE subjects; at Advanced it is intended to represent similar demands to those made on a student taking two A levels, if they complete 12 units, or three A levels if they complete 18. In other words the programmes are intended to appeal to the full ability range and not just to those considered unsuitable for academic courses. The assignments in this book reflect that aim by focusing on complex issues and providing opportunities for the development of a wide range of skills.

The structure of this book is based on the mandatory units required for GNVQ Advanced. Given the considerable overlap in the units at Intermediate and Advanced, however, many of the assignments should prove equally suitable for use at Intermediate.

The leisure and tourism industry

Leisure and tourism is made up of a wide range of very different, but interdependent, activities and operations. These include accommodation, catering, transport, tourist attractions, sport, entertainment, the arts and other recreation and leisure activities. Its economic importance is proved by the fact that in 1991 tourist expenditure in Britain was around £25 billion. Around 7 per cent of employment in Britain is directly related to tourism.

Though leisure and tourism are growing industries in Britain, they are also changing. For example, traditional longer-stay holidays in British destinations are gradually being replaced by more short breaks, second holidays and day trips. Demand for a range of leisure activities has risen, coinciding with the growing awareness of healthier lifestyles. Forecasts suggest that this growth will continue, but will face strong competition from overseas and especially within the single European market.

The implications of this for future planning suggest that improving quality and value for money is of prime importance and that this can only be achieved by increasing standards of training and professionalism. Vocational qualifications have a part to play in creating a more skilled and knowledgeable work force. Schemes such as the Travel and Tourism Programme, supported by American Express, Forte Hotels, The British Tourist Authority/English Tourist Board, along with Thomas Cook, have shown the industry's commitment to improving knowledge, understanding and skills.

The importance of industry links

Though it is not a requirement that teachers of leisure and tourism GNVQ must have worked at some time in a related occupational area, it is essential that local industry links are established. Students are not required to complete a period of work experience either, but their understanding of the issues facing employees in leisure and tourism are likely to be limited if such links are not established. Students have to know what determines business success, what factors it has to cope with which are outside its control and they have to learn how to develop realistic and viable solutions to practical business problems. The advice and experience of outsiders increases the likelihood that what students are learning reflects practice in the industry itself.

Tutor Guide to the Units in Books 1 and 2

Book 1

Unit 1: Investigating the leisure and tourism industry

By comparison with the other seven units, Unit 1 covers potentially a vast amount of ground. Its scope makes it important to be selective in providing or suggesting resources. It would be easy to present students with an overwhelming amount of historical and statistical data which might prove discouraging.

Although there is no requirement to approach the units in a specific order, Unit 1 does contain some fundamental issues, an understanding of which is important at the outset. In particular it deals with definitions of leisure and tourism, as well as with their social, economic, cultural and environmental impacts.

Students may encounter some difficulty in obtaining detailed information about the funding of some leisure and tourism facilities. It is worth checking in advance to find out the extent of the confidentiality of such information.

Unit 2: Maintaining health, safety and security

The intention is that this unit should focus on a specific facility. The assignments cover a number of facilities, however, so that a wider range of issues can be represented. The emphasis on regulation and legislation creates the potential for much very dry reading material. The essential points and applications of relevant legislation to specific work places will be more easily assimilated than the full text of Acts of Parliament or Health and Safety Codes of Practice.

Nevertheless reference to codes of practice and safety standards is necessary and there will be a cost if these are bought from organisations like the Health and Safety Executive or the British Standards Institution.

Unit 3: Providing customer care

Customer care is vital to most parts of the leisure and tourism industry. Many larger organisations use commercially produced training material, such as Video Arts, but others run their own training programmes, and ideas from some of these are incorporated into the assignments.

Though its importance is undeniable, many of the essential principles of customer care are not particularly complex and are common to sectors outside leisure and tourism. The skills involved are often described in very general terms – communication, rapport or efficiency – and these have to be broken down into stages and specific examples. Role plays are particularly useful in showing the relevance of individual skills to particular leisure and tourism contexts.

Unit 4: Marketing in leisure and tourism

This unit focuses on the whole marketing process, from identifying customer needs through to planning promotional campaigns.

In most leisure and tourism businesses marketing is firmly controlled by a budget which may well be based on estimates of future performance. Nor is the process of marketing evaluation always a very exact science. Apart from obvious leaps in sales figures, evaluation may take the form of personal impressions and reports.

Book 2

Unit 5: Planning for an event or function

The events or functions featured in these assignments include both the real and the simulated. The latter sometimes has the advantage of introducing a wider range of issues and constraints into the planning process.

As a planning exercise, this unit encourages group work and problem-solving and should offer the opportunity to develop core skills. The assignments cover extremes of scale, from the national to the local, in order to emphasise both broad planning issues and more specific practical details.

Unit 6: Maintaining information services

Many students will already be familiar with techniques of information handling, especially those using computer technology.

The assignments included reflect both the need for good information services and approaches taken to achieving them in different leisure and tourism contexts.

Dealing with issues of confidentiality and security may prove difficult for some students. For obvious reasons some leisure and tourism businesses are reluctant to release sensitive information, for example about financial performance or personnel. They may permit a teacher or lecturer to 'fictionalise' some data and then allow its use.

Unit 7: Working in teams

The assignments in this unit explore the key principles of team working, as well as looking at some specific examples.

Students should find that research into working practices which they have to do for Units 2, 4 and 8 for example, will enable them to explore how these principles are put into practice in other contexts.

Unit 8: Evaluating the performance of facilities

The depth of evaluation studies carried out in leisure and tourism is often a matter of resources. Where detailed research has been undertaken, professional agencies are often involved.

The assignments reflect the variety of approaches by featuring a very small operation (a guest house) as well as examining aspects of much larger ones like airports or major visitor attractions.

Combination of units and elements

Each of the 8 units is divided into elements, but student activities may cover more than one element at a time. It is equally possible to plan assignments which cover requirements in more than one unit. Research conducted at a single tourist attraction could provide a range of outcomes. For example, Assignments 4.8, 7.1 and 8.1 are all based on Beaulieu. Studying a theme, such as the environmental impact of leisure and tourism, would enable students to establish links between Assignments 1.7, 2.5, 4.5, 5.6 and 8.4. A local study of leisure provision could lead to various combinations of Assignments 1.4, 2.1, 3.3, 4.4 and 6.3.

Core skills

Three core skills are incorporated into GNVQs: Communication, Application of Number and Information Technology. Like most skills, these are best developed in a realistic context; and they are not therefore isolated in this book but are incorporated within the context of a range of assignments.

Because of the nature of their content, some units lend themselves particularly to developing individual core skills. Thus Communication is a vital element in Units 3 and 7, since neither Customer Care nor Working in Teams could exist without it! Similarly Unit 6, Maintaining Information Services, is more dependent on Information Technology skills than some others.

The following examples highlight assignments which could be especially useful in developing core skills:

Communication

Inevitably very few of the assignments do not require the exercise of Communication skills at some point. The following list illustrates the varied approach to developing these:
1.4, 1.7, 1.9, 2.3, 2.5, 2.6, 2.9, 3.2, 3.3, 3.5, 3.7, 4.3, 4.9, 5.1 5.5, 5.9, 6.4, 6.6, 7.1, 7.4, 7.5, 8.4, 8.5, 8.6.

Application of Number

1.1, 2.4, 2.5, 3.1, 3.9, 4.1, 4.2, 4.4, 4.7, 4.9, 5.3, 5.6, 6.7, 7.2, 8.1, 8.2, 8.5, 8.6.

Information Technology

1.11, 6.1, 6.2, 6.3, 6.4, 6.5, 6.8.

In addition Information Technology skills could be applied in the design and presentation of many of the written assignments.

Active learning

These assignments are intended to encourage students to work both on their own and in small groups. Though resource material is provided, it generally also acts as a starting point for further research. The assignments encourage students to develop planning skills, judgement and initiative. Frequent choices are offered and students may wish to add further appropriate options of their own.

The range of activities

These assignments encourage the production of evidence from students in a variety of forms and from a variety of sources. GNVQs encourage the use of investigations, surveys, case studies and planning and designing activities. This book contains many such practical tasks, providing in many cases source material on which they can be wholly or partly based.

Planning and design tasks include the consideration of posters, notices, floor plans, itineraries, business plans, contingency plans and development proposals. The assignments can be used to generate among other things reports, analyses, speeches or presentations, codes of practice and guidance notes. Responses will be written and oral. Students are challenged to identify a range of principles, qualities, changes, arguments and issues relevant to leisure and tourism. The tasks frequently encourage discussion, in small groups and in role, in order to arrive at consensus or to identify a range of conclusions.

Progression

Since research degrees are now awarded for a whole range of leisure and tourism studies, GNVQs provide a number of opportunities for progression. Apart from moving, for example, from Level 2 to Level 3, successful students can move into higher education to follow diploma or degree courses. In some cases it may be possible to combine these with employment, so that the qualification forms part of the individual's overall training.

GNVQ2 Leisure and Tourism: Summary of mandatory units

Unit 1 Investigating leisure and tourism Level 2

1.1 Investigate the leisure and tourism industry in a locality
1.2 Investigate leisure and tourism services and products provided by a facility
1.3 Identify employment opportunities in leisure and tourism

Unit 3 Customer service Level 2

3.1 Investigate the customer care strategies of facilities
3.2 Provide assistance to customers
3.3 Maintain records

Unit 2 Contributing to an event/service Level 2

2.1 Contribute to planning an event/service with others
2.2 Prepare schedules for an event/service with others
2.3 Plan own contribution to a given event/service
2.4 Undertake a role in an event/service with others
2.5 Contribute to the evaluation of an event/service

Unit 4 Promoting products and services Level 2

4.1 Investigate the function of promotion in leisure and tourism
4.2 Evaluate the success of a promotional campaign
4.3 Report on the design of a promotional campaign
4.4 Prepare an outline promotional campaign

GNVQ3 Leisure and Tourism: Summary of mandatory units

Unit 1 Investigating the leisure and tourism industry Level 3

1.1 Describe the scale and contexts of the leisure and tourism industry
1.2 Investigate UK leisure and tourism products
1.3 Investigate the variety of local services and products
1.4 Identify sources of income for leisure and tourism facilities

Unit 5 Planning for an event Level 3

5.1 Propose options for an event
5.2 Present a plan for an event
5.3 Allocate roles and personnel in an event

Unit 2 Maintaining health, safety and security Level 3

2.1 Report on the health, safety, and security arrangements in a facility
2.2 Propose ways of enhancing the health and safety of customers and staff
2.3 Propose ways of enhancing security in leisure and tourism

Unit 6 Providing management information services Level 3

6.1 Plan a management information service
6.2 Select and provide management information
6.3 Record and process management information

Unit 3 Providing customer service Level 3

3.1 Identify the function of customer service in leisure and tourism facilities
3.2 Plan a customer care programme
3.3 Provide customer service
3.4 Evaluate the operation of the customer care programme

Unit 7 Working in teams Level 3

7.1 Investigate how leisure and tourism work teams operate
7.2 Work with others in teams
7.3 Evaluate team performance

Unit 4 Marketing in leisure and tourism Level 3

4.1 Identify market needs for products and services
4.2 Identify market opportunities
4.3 Plan promotional activities
4.4 Evaluate promotional activities

Unit 8 Evaluating the performance of facilities Level 3

8.1 Research the organisational objectives of facilities
8.2 Plan the evaluation of a facility's performance
8.3 Evaluate the performance of a facility

Mandatory units for General National Vocational Qualifications offered by Business and Technology Education Council, City and Guilds and RSA Examinations Board from September 1993

Acknowledgements

The author and publishers would like to thank the following organisations for permission to reproduce photographs and other material:

The Commonwealth Institute (page 2); Princes Risborough Photographic Society (page 6); English Tourist Board (pages 9, 10, 68); The Brewery (page 15); Alton Towers (pages 21, 89, 90); Forte (pages 27 and 57); Performe Publications (pages 33–4); Unipart Group of Companies (page 36); Beaulieu (pages 49, 60, 72); Yorkshire Mining Museum (page 74) and for the cover photographs Tony Stone Images and The Telegraph Colour Library. All other photographs were supplied by the author.

Every effort has been made to contact copyright holders and we apologise if any have been overlooked.

The Travel and Tourism Programme

An interesting feature of leisure and tourism is its increasing recognition of the importance of education as a means of encouraging young people, teachers and parents to give consideration to what is rapidly becoming the world's largest industrial sector.

Students are being encouraged to view the industries both from the standpoint of discriminating consumers and as career options. With the aim of fostering this dual perspective, the Travel and Tourism Programme, supported by American Express, Forte Hotels, and the British Tourist Authority/English Tourist Board, along with Thomas Cook, has willingly enabled these materials to be written.

John Ward is Professional Officer with the Travel and Tourism Programme.

Unit 5 Planning for an event or function

5.1 Planning a festival: Commonwealth Day

Develops knowledge and understanding of the following element:
I   Propose options for an event

Supports the development of the following core skills:
Communication level 3: Take part in discussions (Tasks 1, 2, 3)

Each year, during the early part of March, the Commonwealth Institute in London holds a Commonwealth Day. This event, first proposed by the Canadian Prime Minister Pierre Trudeau, is held in Commonwealth countries worldwide on the same day. The way in which it is organised reflects the main objective of the event: to celebrate the many different cultures of the 50 countries belonging to the Commonwealth. Children are encouraged to experience some of the sights, sounds and traditions of other countries. The festival builds on the underlying principle that greater international understanding is essential if world problems such as famine, disease, environmental damage and wars are ever to be eliminated.

The content of the Commonwealth Day Programme has to address two needs: how to make the Commonwealth better known to children and how to give each year's activities an interesting and topical focus. The first issue is partly met by the permanent exhibitions from all the Commonwealth countries on show within the Institute. These are supplemented on the day itself by the presence of representatives of those countries, usually members of the staff of their High Commissions. The second need is met by choosing a theme for each year's festival. Past Commonwealth Days have focused on such themes as sport, women in the Commonwealth, the Commonwealth view of Columbus and on new members of the Commonwealth such as Pakistan and Namibia. The use of a different theme each year adds variety but is also important for another reason. Children may find the principle of a Commonwealth too broad to grasp; concentrating on a particular theme may make this easier to understand.

Planning an event of this size requires agreement both about individual responsibilities and about the timetable for completing each stage of the preparations. Once the theme has been agreed, letters have to be sent to all High Commissioners requesting their co-operation. Some may need to be persuaded. The best ways of encouraging their participation or that of their staff is to stress the past success of the event and to offer guidance about what they might actually do. They can be encouraged to wear national dress, to teach children some words of their language and to distribute some information. Bringing too much to hand out to children may prove unhelpful in that it creates congestion in some areas of the exhibition hall. One way of avoiding congestion is to assign groups of students specific countries whose displays they must visit first.

If the event is to run smoothly, children need to be prepared for it as well as other participants. Those who intend to visit are sent advance notes explaining what the Commonwealth is and providing some background about the current year's theme. Guidance is offered about courtesy towards Commonwealth representatives, some of whom may be senior diplomats. The notes also contain some questions which children might like to ask about individual countries or about the festival theme. Teachers need information about the charge for attendance and advice about the best ways of getting to the Institute.

The Commonwealth Institute premises are open to the public all year round and so particular care has to be taken to ensure that the building itself can accommodate the event successfully. Parts of the building can be privately hired, so one of the first tasks in organising Commonwealth Day is to book all the required spaces – for example galleries, the lecture theatre and the lawn – well in advance. It is also important to know the number of staff who will be available to help on the day, in case extra part-time workers have to be hired. Fire regulations have to be checked to make sure that acceptable safety limits are set in terms of the numbers of visitors admitted overall and to individual areas like the film theatre.

A quantity of tickets and forms will have to be designed, made and distributed. When decisions are made about furniture layout, car parking arrangements, audio-visual aids, and artefacts to be delivered and exhibited, information about the arrangements agreed has to be sent to all personnel who will be affected. In the case of valuable artefacts, particularly where they are going to be handled by children, it may be necessary to arrange special insurance cover. Signs also have to be made and decisions taken about where these should be positioned. They need to be of good quality so that they both create a favourable impression of the occasion and also convey directional information clearly.

Generally the festival involves a number of events and performances. These need to be appropriate to the theme and, in the case of performances, they need to be monitored to ensure the quality and reliability of the performers. Events, such as the release of helium-

Commonwealth Day at The Commonwealth Institute

filled balloons bearing the names of all the Commonwealth countries, need to have the right resources in the right place at the right time if they are to run smoothly.

Parallel to all this preparation is the marketing effort: Commonwealth Day will not be perceived as a great success if very few children turn up! The Institute has a Press Officer who will contact the media. Having a themed event is an advantage here in that journalists have a more obvious focus for a story. When a reassessment of Columbus was the theme in 1992, television news featured a school rap group taking part in the Commonwealth Day performance. Information about the festival is mailed to all schools.

Your tasks

Below is a draft timetable for Commonwealth Day Festival 1993.

Commonwealth Day Festival 1993   March 8th 1993

9.30	High Commission representatives arrive, set up displays and/or tables and have coffee with staff
10.00	Visit the Commonwealth – school groups have the chance to visit every country in the Commonwealth while remaining under one roof... ...and to visit displays of work on this year's theme of *Human Values* brought by participating schools
11.45	Official opening by guest Commonwealth speaker, followed by dance/drama performances
12.30	Selected visitors proceed to lawn for balloon release
12.40	Balloon release
12.55	Director General's reception for High Commission representatives and other invited guests

Note: The theme for 1993 is Human Values and may touch on some or all of the following:
- legal, political and individual rights and whether these are equitably distributed
- the equal distribution of social and economic rights
- ecological and environmental rights, especially of future generations.

1 Write the text of a letter to be sent to all High Commissioners inviting them to participate in the 1993 Commonwealth Day Festival.

2 Write the text of a letter to be sent to all schools inviting them to apply to attend the 1993 Festival.

3 Propose an event or function to take place in your own locality to celebrate Commonwealth Day.

5.2 Organising a national festival

Develops knowledge and understanding of the following element:
1   Propose options for an event

Supports the development of the following core skills:
Communication level 3: Take part in discussions (Task 1)
Communication level 3: Prepare written material (Task 2)
Communication level 3: Read and respond to written material and images (Task 3)

One of the first tasks given to the new government Department of National Heritage, when it was set up in early 1992, was to organise a European arts festival in Britain.

It was planned in the three-month period preceding its six month lifespan, from July to September 1992. A government grant of £6 million enabled some 1000 events to be staged at 250 different venues. Events included operatic performances, an arts trail, international theatre productions and a laser sculpture exhibition. The geographical spread of the events covered the whole of the United Kingdom.

The short time available for planning such a complex event meant that a number of organisations were approached for support. Regional Tourist Boards, the Arts Council and local authorities all suggested projects which might make appropriate contributions to the festival as a whole. These included new projects, as well as some which were already in existence but which could be enhanced by additional funding. Some event organisers wished to bring them under the wing of the festival, regardless of whether financial support was likely to be forthcoming.

The festival's main objective was to celebrate the United Kingdom's contribution to Europe's cultural heritage. Underlying that, however, was a desire to attract more people to develop an interest in the arts. The planners believed that young people especially received too little exposure to the arts and that much potential interest was therefore lost.

Two specific ways of meeting these broad objectives were tried. Educational and entertainment programmes in a variety of media formed the basis of a travelling exhibition which visited a number of less accessible locations around the UK. Publicity about the festival was mailed to 35 000 schools and 250 of the festival's events were intended to appeal specifically to young people.

The main problem faced by the festival organisers was the matter of publicising it effectively. It is much easier to advertise a one-week annual musical festival in a single town than it is to make people aware of a six-month programme spread around the whole country. An example of the problem is that public libraries have been used to distribute publicity material. However this means events are more likely to attract existing arts enthusiasts. They are less likely to come to the attention of the potential new audience which the festival planners originally had in mind.

Your tasks

1 Discuss which areas of the United Kingdom might have limited direct access to the arts.

a) Allocate a specific location to each student.

b) Identify a specific social issue to which a national organisation might wish to give wider publicity.

c) Assume that it has been decided that the best means of making an impact in the locations allocated is by drawing attention to the issue through all or some of the following:
- painting and sculpture
- dance
- drama
- literature
- music
- film.

Funds totalling £50 000 have been allocated to this particular venture.

Write a list of objectives for an arts event intended to have just such an impact.

2 Suggest three different schemes which would meet the objectives listed in Task 1. Each suggestion should explain the following:
- the format of the event
- how people would be encouraged to atttend
- what resources would be needed
- what the likely costs would be.

3 Prepare a short presentation outlining each of the three schemes and explaining, with reasons, which one would be most likely to achieve the main objectives proposed.

5.3 Government funding for sport in the community

Develops knowledge and understanding of the following element:

I   Propose options for an event

Supports the development of the following core skills:

Application of number level 3: Gather and process data (Task 1)
Communication level 3: Use images to illustrate points made in writing and discussion (Task 2)
Communication level 3: Take part in discussions (Tasks 3, 4)

In 1972 a Royal Charter established the Sports Council as an independent body whose main objectives were to increase participation in sport, to raise standards of performance, and to improve the quality and quantity of sports facilities. The Council is supported by a grant from the Government, although it also raises money from other sources.

5

Government sponsorship aims to encourage less traditional sports.

The Council is heavily involved in supporting coaching events in a wide range of sports. As part of its drive to make more facilities available to the community it has encouraged the opening up of more school facilities to the public, providing lighting and introducing artificial surfaces. It also produces research into the long-term demand for facilities and the effect of outreach work on socially disadvantaged groups.

In 1992 the Government announced further financial support to encourage the spread of sport in the community. £3 million has been contributed towards a sponsorship scheme called Sportsmatch. This scheme deliberately ignores national events and focuses on those planned for young people, especially those who might already be facing some sort of social disadvantage.

Planned sporting events which meet the criteria, and which do not already have an existing sponsorship arrangement, can apply for grants of up to £75 000, provided that they can find businesses which are willing to match the sum they are seeking. The intention of the scheme is to encourage financial support for sports other than the traditional ones which already appeal to spectators and hence are attractive to sponsors. One advantage of the scheme is that the support from businesses does not have to be cash. Their contribution can be through the provision of equipment, support services or rent-free premises.

Money for community sport also comes from local government, though their responsibility is largely the provision of facilities rather than of events. They may be willing to give financial support to national sporting events if they believe these will bring prestige or income to the region.

The issue which is often forgotten in debates about the funding of sport is the fact that the Government actually derives a significant income from it. Recent figures suggested it received £3.56 billion from a combination of sporting sources including VAT, income tax and National Insurance, excise and betting duty and corporation tax. This figure is claimed to be nearly seven times the amount spent by the Government on sport. Given the recorded growth of active participation in sport, many argue that government investment in it should be greater.

Your tasks

1 Conduct local research to establish which three sports, for which local facilities are not currently available, would be most attractive to the local community.

2 Plan a demonstration and/or coaching event intended both to give the community a chance to learn more about these sports and also to assess whether there is local talent or potential which deserves to be developed.

3 Make a presentation outlining each of your three proposals and addressing the following issues:
- objectives
- staffing
- sources of funding
- costs and income generated by the event itself
- safety
- publicity
- potential take-up and capacity
- follow up.

4 Appoint a different panel, made up of three students, for each presentation. Their task is to select the best of the three options and to justify their choice.

5.4 Planning a public meeting about a leisure development

Develops knowledge and understanding of the following element:
I   Propose options for an event

Supports the development of the following core skills:
Communication level 3: Prepare written material (Task 1)
Communication level 3: Take part in discussions (Task 2)

The village of Lesser Elthorne, on the outskirts of Easthampton, has no leisure facilities of its own. Approaches have been made to the Parish Council by a leisure development company, Downer Hill Associates, about converting the eastern slope of Elthorne Hill into a dry ski slope.

The company prospectus makes the following claims:

'Skiing is the most exciting way to keep fit. Imagine yourself, knees bent, trees flashing by and finally waving gracefully to spectators as you describe a graceful curve at the end of your run. What's more, you no longer have to go all the way to Switzerland to do it! With Downer Hill Associates' knowledge and expertise such thrills can literally be on your doorstep. Give your community what it needs - fun and fitness at a very competitive price.'

Easthampton Town Planning Department, approached by a journalist from the Easthampton Recorder, offered the following remarks, while making it clear that no formal approach had been made by Downer Hill Associates:

"These slopes can use existing terrain but can considerably change the visual appearance of a site where substantial amounts of earth have to be moved. Elthorne Hill is traversed by a footpath popular with dog walkers and there is a good view of the village from the top of the hill. Even if permission were to be granted, the developers have to be very careful to check that the site is actually suitable. It has not been established that a ski slope will attract sufficient users or whether it is intended to combine it with another facility like a restaurant. Skiing may have only a seasonal appeal, being much more popular between September and March.'

There is a plan to cut staff and reduce services at Easthampton General Hospital. When the idea of the development was raised in a radio interview with the hospital manager, she gave the following warning:

'You will get all types of skiers, from the novices who need gentle slopes to the experts who may require much more challenging inclines and undulations. The accident risks are high. Artificial ski surfaces are usually made from plastic. Friction between skis and the surface, however, and the varied weather conditions we get in the United Kingdom mean that inferior surfaces wear very quickly and become hazardous if they are not replaced, a costly business. While real snow may cushion a fall to some extent, artificial surfaces can cause burns, cuts, broken bones and torn clothing. Our emergency and accident department is already over-worked and would be unlikely to welcome the scheme.'

The residents of Lesser Elthorne have mixed feelings about the possible development. A number, and not just the younger ones, feel that the community suffers from the lack of local leisure facilities. Shop owners especially wish to reverse the trend of villagers going into Easthampton for leisure and shopping purposes, also hoping that a ski slope would bring outsiders with money to spend into the village.

There is certainly some concern about the possible effects of the slope on the appearance of Elthorne Hill. A local builder expressed some of his fears:

'There are many things which can go wrong in the construction of these slopes. Drainage can be a problem, particularly if the site has not been inspected to check its state at the time of year when weather conditions are at their worst. It is vital to prepare the ground thoroughly before laying down the artificial surface since any lumps will make the top surface dangerous. The gradients should be carefully checked too, to make sure they are neither too steep nor too gentle. All of this will require the movement of a considerable amount of earth, a noisy, dirty and inconvenient process. What's more, the elevation of Elthorne Hill means that ski lifts and any construction at the top of the slope will be visible from most parts of the village.'

Your tasks

It is decided to hold a public meeting to debate the potential of the ski slope proposal.

1 List the objectives which this meeting should attempt to meet.

2 Propose three alternative approaches to planning the meeting, including:
- its structure
- its contents and participants
- the methods of inviting its audience.

Given that feelings are running high in the village, work in small groups to agree which of the three options prepared by each student would be most likely to fulfil the meeting's objectives.

5.5 Planning activity holidays

Develops knowledge and understanding of the following element:
2   Present a plan for an event

Supports the development of the following core skills:
Communication level 3: Take part in discussions, Read and respond to written material
         and images (Task 1)
Communication level 3: Prepare written material (Task 2)

Perhaps as a reaction to too many holidays spent lying on a beach or sitting in a deckchair or perhaps because of warnings about the dangers of too much exposure to the sun, in recent years there has been a marked growth in the popularity of activity holidays.

Planning a new activity holiday requires attention to a wide range of details. Activity holidays carry a higher degree of risk than most others, though there are clearly varying degrees of danger involved. For example, mountaineering is more dangerous than walking, but perhaps safer than hang-gliding.

Many activity centres cater for children and so the quality of the staff they employ is very important. They should have a means of checking that the staff have no previous record of mistreating children in any way. They will also need to demonstrate a high level of skills and an acceptable knowledge of first aid procedures.

Activity centres should be required to record all accidents, including a full explanation of how they happened. Evidence suggests that many accidents to children actually happen during free time. This raises questions about what the correct amount of supervision should be.

Two types of activity holiday which carry particular risks of injury are pony-trekking and water sports. The hot summers of 1990 and 1991 led to an increase of algae in many

Many activity centres cater for children and the quality of the staff is of great importance.

stretches of fresh water. Anyone swallowing any of this could suffer very serious after effects. Yet there is no legal requirement for staff at activity centres to have first aid qualifications.

The Department for Education has published a document called 'Safety in Outdoor Pursuits' which recommends safety procedures for all centres involved in activity holidays. Most Local Education Authorities also have their own sets of guidelines. The ratio of leaders or instructors to students is an important factor in any safety policy. The training and qualifications of those instructors should also be open to inspection. Many activities are reliant on equipment and this needs to be of a high standard and to be regularly inspected. If you are abseiling down a cliff you want to feel confident that the rope won't break!

Activity holiday equipment needs to be of a high standard and regularly inspected.

Skiing holidays carry a much higher risk of injury than most. The most common injuries suffered are pulled muscles and twisted joints, though broken limbs are not unknown of course. The likelihood of such injuries occurring could be reduced if holiday-makers were to follow a training programme aimed at improving their fitness before they set off. Falls can be caused by incompetence but fatigue is also often a factor. Pre-holiday exercises in the form of running or cycling can improve the stamina of potential skiers and so lessen the chances of falls resulting from tiredness.

Any plan for an activity holiday scheme should take account of its likely impact on the environment. Some kinds of activity holiday are creating concern because of the impact of new developments on vulnerable environments. Skiing in the Alps is perhaps the best known example. Skiing has grown so rapidly in the area that it is estimated that there are now some 40 000 ski runs and 14 000 ski lifts.

Skiing is totally dependent on snow. In years when there is not enough ski resorts have started to rely on artificial snow machines. Compressed air and water are sprayed at high pressure when temperatures are below feezing. This creates extra snow but is a serious drain on the local water supply. Some methods of making artificial snow also use chemicals to speed the formation of ice crystals. The use of snow machines also means that the skiing season can be extended. This can affect the habitat of local wildlife. It can also increase the damage to the slopes themselves, particularly if people ski over muddy patches. This can accelerate soil erosion and damage wild flowers.

However it is the construction of new ski resorts which perhaps gives the greatest cause for concern. In order to produce suitable ski runs thousands of trees are cleared.

Slopes are reshaped, often involving the movement of thousands of tons of earth and the blasting of rocks. This can noticeably increase the dangers from avalanches, since trees give some protection. It has meant that many Alpine roads are covered by a succession of unsightly concrete avalanche shelters. The steel pylons, overhead cables, lifts and tows which are necessary in ski resorts are also visually unattractive.

The construction of new golf courses raises similar concerns. Trees are cut down and earth moved in vast quantities to create hazards. In order to keep the fairways and greens usable, a huge daily supply of water is sprayed over courses in hotter climates. Recent television pictures showed a drought in Zimbabwe, while golf courses in the same country continued to use sprinkler systems. In the United Kingdom, as elsewhere, herbicides and fertilisers are used in large quantities to keep the grass healthy. The result is often a build up of phosphates which eventually drain off into nearby water, increasing algae growth and suffocating fish and other wildlife.

A proposed new activity centre must undergo a feasibility study. Developing a new golf course is seen as an attractive option by leisure developers at the moment, partly because changes in agricultural policy have led farmers to seek alternative uses for land formerly used for cultivation or grazing. In some parts of the country golf clubs have long waiting lists for membership and so there appears to be considerable demand for such facilities. Developers may even get grants to support this change of land use. Some people think this is often a short cut to gaining planning permission for additional building around the course, such as club houses, hotels and apartments. It might be more difficult to gain planning permission to build these in the countryside without the initial construction of a golf course.

Purchasing land or property is often the major cost for companies intending to establish new activity centres. Before deciding to go ahead with such a purchase, however, the company has to establish whether there is sufficient demand for the facilities it intends to provide. The fact that there are waiting lists at most private golf clubs and that you have to book well in advance on many public courses is taken as evidence that there is considerable demand for more golf courses. Yet there would be little point in constructing one which was several hours' drive from the nearest population centre.

In most developments financial backing will be required. The type of development will probably determine how interested investors are. While there may be interest in golf courses with large hotels, intending to attract high-spending business clients, it is more difficult to get funding for municipal courses open to the general public.

The construction of a golf course illustrates the range of costs which have to be met by developers of activity centres. The construction costs involved will depend on the existing terrain. Natural drainage, for example, will save expenditure on ditches and drainage and water systems. Access roads and car parks will need to be put in, as will power supplies and a sewerage system. Some golf centres will also include space-consuming practice facilities, such as driving ranges or putting practice areas. Grants or loans to meet some of these costs are sometimes available from interested sports bodies. However, the majority of the funding is generally raised by persuading other companies to invest in the scheme.

Income once a golf course is operating comes mainly from the fees paid by players, or membership fees as well if the club is private. Many courses cater for more than 50 000 rounds of golf a year and they need to keep players moving reasonably rapidly round the course if they are not to lose money during the course of the year. Driving ranges, which can be completed fairly quickly after planning permission has been granted, are sometimes used to generate income while a new golf course is being constructed elsewhere on the same site.

Your tasks

1 Suppose that you have to organise a party of twenty twelve-year-olds to undertake a cliff top walk.

Below is a list of ten rules which you might draw up for the party to follow. However, some of them would probably be more useful than others. Discuss which six rules you think would be most likely to ensure the safety of your party.

---

1 Always walk in pairs, holding hands.
2 Do not go closer than ten metres to the cliff's edge, unless you are following a path protected on the seaward side by a good fence or wall.
3 Check that you are wearing sensible walking shoes, particularly avoiding high heels or flip-flops.
4 Allow no talking at any time.
5 Make sure that two or more adults are supervising the group at all times.
6 Allow the quicker walkers to go ahead at their own pace.
7 Take a lightweight rucksack for sandwiches, drinks and emergency rations.
8 Do not leave the marked footpath, unless a section of it appears sufficiently damaged to be dangerous.
9 Take along a football for a bit of entertainment along the route.
10 Carry a detailed local map and a compass, and tell a responsible person of your intended route.

---

2 Draw up a similar set of safety rules for a sponsored walk taking in both a canal towpath and a main road.

5.6 Renovating a children's playground: resource requirements

Develops knowledge and understanding of the following element:
2 Present a plan for an event

Supports the development of the following core skills:
Application of number level 3: Represent and tackle problems (Task 1)
Communication level 3: Prepare written material; Application of number level 3: Represent and tackle problems (Task 2)

Any event put on for children is likely to require special attention to any play equipment they are likely to use. On the one hand there may be a desire to provide the safest environment, including such items as impact absorbent floors. On the other hand the available budget may mean that a certain amount of improvisation is necessary in order to provide acceptable resources at affordable costs.

The people of Oldcliffe-by-the-Sea decided, as part of their annual village festival, to hold a Children's Fair. There was a dilapidated playground, part of the now-closed village school, which the Festival Committee was proposing to restore to full use and to open formally on the day of the Festival.

The first task was to inspect the existing equipment, consisting of two sets of three swings, a slide, a roundabout and a small climbing frame. All metal supports were examined for signs of corrosion. The bases of supports and the areas where they were set into the ground were closely examined and a number of repairs implemented and thoroughly tested. Some parts of the equipment were held together by bolts. These were individually checked, replaced where necessary and firmly tightened.

Years of disuse had resulted in considerable vandalism. Litter, glass and graffiti were removed. All surfaces, such as swing seats, the roundabout top and the slide chute were inspected for sharp edges and splinters. These were first made safe and then thoroughly cleaned.

Most of the ground immediately surrounding the equipment was concrete. The frame of one of the sets of swings was found to be badly twisted. Though it might have lasted for a year or two, it would eventually prove costly to replace. Since consideration of the cost of providing a softer floor covering to go over the concrete was proving a problem, it was decided to remove this set of swings altogether and concentrate on having one safe set in good working order. However, the age of the existing swings meant that the frame was higher than more modern designs. The result of this was that children could potentially fall from greater heights and fall further distances than with a lower structure. It was eventually decided that it would cost less to provide a wider area of soft flooring than it would to replace the swings with newer ones.

All the metal parts of the playground equipment were painted. Surface corrosion was first descaled. The roundabout was dismantled and all the moving parts serviced. Quantities of rubbish were removed from underneath it at the same time. This raised further questions about what kind of floor surface would be appropriate. Choices included soft material derived from bark and wood planings. This had the advantage of providing a good grip underfoot whatever the weather conditions. Further advantages were that it would prove cheaper than some other surfaces and would drain fairly easily. However, because the playground area was not completely flat it would have needed regular raking. Heavy wear in the areas closest to the equipment would also have quickly made the surface uneven. Some members of the Committee argued that this type of surface would eventually rot unless extra drainage was installed. This meant that although rubberised systems were more expensive they were likely to last longer and require less maintenance. In the end they opted for a system using polyurethane, which was poured just into the areas surrounding the playground equipment, to provide a softer surface.

Your tasks

1 The playground was surrounded on three sides by 90 metres of wire fencing attached to wooden posts. However, this had been flattened in a number of places and about half the posts were badly rotted. The wall of the school building provided a safe and secure barrier on the fourth side.

Work out the full relative costs of repairing the fence against the costs of replacing it with any one of two or three alternative styles of barriers.

Taking into account the purpose of such a barrier, its likely wear and tear, and the relative costs of the various ways of getting it erected, write a brief report for the Festival Committee suggesting what approach you think they should take.

2 The top of the existing slide stands some 3 metres above ground level. There is a handrail up both sides of the steps supported by metal rods at intervals of 30 centimetres. There is just a handrail on the small platform at the top. The sides of the chute are raised 20 centimetres and at the foot of the descent the sliding surface extends on a level plane for 5 metres.

Write a brief report for the Festival Committee describing whether or not you think this slide is safe. Your report might suggest modifications and/or the erection of a warning notice.

5.7 Planning a conference – the need for a schedule

Develops knowledge and understanding of the following element:
2   Present a plan for an event

Supports the development of the following core skills:
Communication level 3: Prepare written material (Task 1)
Communication level 3: Take part in discussions (Task 2)

Conference business has become an important part of the hospitality industry. Larger hotels regard conferences as opportunities to attract a guaranteed number of customers for a period known well in advance. Many attractions, aware of the appeal of their distinctive environments, have developed conference facilities. Some industrial sites with the advantage of city centre locations, like The Whitbread Brewery in London, have converted former business premises for use as conference centres.

The success of a conference has much to do with the liaison which has taken place at the planning stage between the company or organisation involved and those who manage the venue itself. This usually requires the recognition of a single person as the point of contact for the company and another for the venue. Once they have agreed the format of the event, they can then allocate and delegate responsibility for individual areas and formulate a timing plan.

At The Brewery an Account Manager will be appointed to work with each new client. They will initially discuss an agreed timescale, similar to the following example:

1 The client visits the venue to be advised of its full potential
2 A provisional booking made - to be held up to 14 days
3 The booking is confirmed in writing
4 A contract outlining the terms of the booking is sent out
5 The contract is signed and returned with a deposit payment

6 A liaison meeting between Account Manager and client to agree conference details is held 2–3 weeks before the actual event

7 An Event Reservation form is sent to the client

8 Any final changes are discussed

9 The client provides a provisional list of attenders 10 days before the event

10 Final numbers and any seating plan requirements are indicated by the client 3 days before the event.

However, planning a conference is not just about hiring a suitable venue. Much work may have to be done in organising the list of delegates, in supplying them with information about both the conference and the venue, and, most important of all, in making sure that the overall purpose and message of the conference is successfully delivered.

Larger conferences may involve inviting delegates from a number of different companies and regions, as well as a number of guest speakers. The timing of invitations is important, particularly where the people in question are very busy or much in demand as public speakers. Decisions about whether or not to attend may be dependent on other things besides dates. The quality of the information available about the conference may attract or deter potential delegates. The status of the team actually delivering the conference, as well as the guest speakers they have been able to attract, will also influence attendance.

Even where a conference is limited to a particular company and attendance is not voluntary, delegates need to be provided with clear information in advance. This is often produced in a folder which will give details of the conference programme, directions to and around the conference venue and details of restaurants and attractions nearby. Sometimes a list of suggested reading might be included. Many conferences break up the possible monotony of a succession of lectures by including sessions where delegates have to opt for different topics or where they are divided into discussion or work groups. The information pack can help the conference to run more smoothly by giving advanced knowledge of the make-up of working groups or by including return slips asking delegates to nominate the optional sessions they would like to be involved in. If delegates are unlikely to know a number of others attending the conference, name badges can be included with the information folder.

The conference centre at The Whitbread Brewery, London

Ensuring that the delegates get the right message from the conference is more difficult. If the presenters and guest speakers are outsiders, it is important to have first-hand experience of how effective they are. It is also vital that they are aware of the intended message of the conference since, otherwise, they may make a very professional but totally irrelevant contribution. Though it is the content of the presenters which is most important, their impact can be reinforced or weakened by the quality of equipment and audio-visual aids available to support them. All equipment has to be tested, on the day it is needed, in the room in which it is to be used. Larger venues will probably have technical specialists on site to advise on equipment, sound and lighting.

Other ways in which the conference message can be put across include using company logos and messages on the conference stationery, using sets designed to emphasise the main theme and including entertainment and social activities designed to make delegates feel the whole event is both well thought out and enjoyable. Small details, like the availability of soft drinks and sweets during conference sessions or the presence of flowers on the tables, can also point to the importance which the organisers attach to the conference.

Your tasks

Identify an area of your school/college which could be used for a conference.

1   Prepare a leaflet advertising the venue and explaining the terms of use and the facilities available. You should take into consideration the number and type of staff required, existing regulations and letting arrangements, safety measures and the provision and operation of resources and equipment.

2   Investigate the feasibility of putting on the following conference proposal in your school or college:

A one-day conference for lecturers in travel and tourism

This conference, on the subject of General National Vocational Qualifications, is expected to attract 60 delegates. At this time the qualification is a new one and the conference organisers want the day to be informative, as well as stimulating interest in the new courses.

A reception area will be needed, staffed by someone able to register delegates and provide any information they lack.

Four guest speakers have been invited, two of whom will come by car and two who will need to be met at a station. Microphones will be required and one speaker wishes to illustrate her talk with slides. A 15-minute video also forms part of the morning programme, which will be split up by a coffee break in the middle.

Lunch will be provided for delegates. In the afternoon they will be split into four discussion groups, requiring separate rooms. After a tea break they will return to the main conference room for a question and answer session.

Display tables for free literature are needed, as is space for up to six publishers to exhibit books and resources about travel and tourism during the lunch interval and at the end of the afternoon.

Prepare a short presentation explaining your conclusions and showing how resources in your school or college could be deployed to meet these requirements successfully.

5.8 Hiring premises

Develops knowledge and understanding of the following element:
2   Present a plan for an event

Supports the development of the following core skills:
Communication level 3: Read and respond to written material and images (Task 1)
Communication level 3: Prepare written material (Task 2)

Any indoor event or function organiser will have to be fully aware of the conditions which apply when they book premises for the occasion. These will usually cover issues like payment, times, types of use, access, insurance, cancellation charges and damage claims.

When a booking is made and confirmed in writing, this usually means the event organisers and the venue owners have entered into a contract. The owners may reserve the right not to accept the booking, particularly if they think it is an inappropriate use of the premises. The owners of a stately home which can be booked for banquets might turn down an application to hold a rugby club dinner. A local authority might turn down an application from a political or pressure group, especially if they thought the occasion might provoke unrest. The application might also be rejected if the numbers involved seemed likely to exceed recommended safety levels.

Once the contract has been entered into, it sometimes proves necessary to cancel the event or function. Hiring agreements, rather like many holiday bookings, may stipulate cancellation charges. These are usually dependent on the length of notice which is given and are often calculated on a percentage of what the full hiring charge would have been. For example a major conference venue might ask for 25 per cent of the agreed fee to be paid if a cancellation takes place six months before the agreed date, but 90 per cent if notification arrives two weeks before hand. If an alternative booking is secured for the same date, the cancellation charge is generally forgotten. Larger venues will normally insist on their right to cancel the booking without any liability in certain extreme circumstances. These would include things like fire or industrial action.

The agreement will usually include information about the level of charges and how and when these are to be paid. The cost to the hirers may consist simply of a flat fee, but if the event is a complex one, there may also be unspecified charges for food and the supply of materials and services. A deposit is usually required to secure a booking with the remaining sums becoming due after the event, when the venue owners send out an invoice for the amount still owed.

Larger venues may have their own regulations about acceptable use. Permission may have to be sought for things like fixing posters to the walls or setting up a stage set. Some activities, such as the showing of films, may require a licence under the Cinema Act; the venue may not be in possession of one. Licences would also be required if it was proposed to have alcohol on sale and if a dance or live music were proposed as part of the programme.

Larger events and functions present some security problems. They attract large numbers of people and yet many will be unfamiliar to each other, making it easy for outsiders to go unnoticed. Event organisers are usually held responsible for property loss or damage to property of people attending the function. Venue owners will often state in their written conditions of hire that they accept no responsibility or liability for loss or damage, unless they have specifically agreed to store equipment in a secure place. The conditions may also state that any damage caused by participants will also render them liable to recompense the owners.

The event organisers would probably be required to provide public liability insurance. This would cover them against any costs incurred if legal proceedings were taken against them as the result of an injury or loss or damage to property suffered by anyone participating in the event. Larger venues, catering for bigger events, may insist on a minimum amount of insurance cover.

The conditions of use may also cover a number of safety and security issues. Where a complex electrical operation is needed, for example for a theatrical performance, there may be rules about safety fittings, power connections and cable routes. There will probably be fire regulations to comply with, insisting that fire exit signs are kept clearly visible, extinguishers remain accessible and exits and gangways are kept free from obstruction. Smoking may be banned in some areas. For events which require hired contractors to set them up beforehand, the venue owners may insist on security passes being issued to all bona fide workers.

Your tasks

A travelling theatre company wishes to stage a public performance in your school or college.

1 Draw up a list of terms and conditions of hire which the company must agree to before they are permitted to hire your premises.
  You may need to consult regulations already established by your school or college governing body.

2 Contact either an individual performer or a dance, drama or music group.
  Send them a copy of your terms and conditions, and a letter asking them to comment on the feasibility of using the premises on these terms and conditions. Discuss their responses.

5.9 Planning schedules

Develops knowledge and understanding of the following element:

2   Present a plan for an event

Supports the development of the following core skills:

Communication level 3: Use images to illustrate points made in writing and discussion
    (Tasks 1, 2, 3)

Planning events of any size requires extensive consultation. This will generally begin on an informal basis but once there is agreement that the event should take place more formal meetings have to be held. In addition to the organisation of the event itself there may need to be consultation with outside agencies such as the police, the local authority and the fire service. Larger events, such as festivals, are often managed by committees. Sometimes smaller sub-groups are appointed to plan specific tasks.

Below is an extract from a report written in 1978, describing a suggested sequence of planning stages for a committee organising a festival, commemoration or anniversary:

Festival Planning Report

1 Form small initial group for early discussion and making provisional outline of project
2 Consult local Regional Tourist Board and Local Authorities
3 Form official Management Committee and ensure membership includes necessary skills in law, finance and insurance and representatives of appropriate sections of community. Consider possibility Superior Council to determine policy and/or patrons of substantial local or national stature. Consider how work can be divided and decision-making efficiency improved by formation of sub-committees.
4 Consider possible sources of funds from private donations, grants or guarantees from commercial and industrial communities, Local Authorities, official tourist bodies, Arts Council of Great Britain (see point 7 below), etc. In the light of plans made (see point 5 below) estimate total expenditure and sum to be recouped, i.e. net cost.
5 Make plans for nature, scale and length of celebrations which may have to be modified in the light of financial and other support which can be reasonably expected. Relate plans to availability of halls, theatres, weather expectation, hotel accommodation, catering and transport facilities, etc.
6 Consider whether project justifies or needs engagement of professionals for artistic direction, management, performances, publicity, public relations, etc.
7 Consider whether the cultural and artistic element of the celebration justifies applying for financial support from the Arts Council of Great Britain, or, alternatively, from the Scottish, Welsh or Northern Ireland Arts Councils or one of the regional Arts Associations.
8 Consider whether the benefit to the public justifies application for registration as a charity with consequent tax advantages particularly when continuing existence envisaged.
9 Consider whether scale and nature of operations contemplated suggest formation of company incorporated with financial liability.
10 Make certain there is adequate insurance against accident and other risks.
11 begin promotional publicity early: Leaflets, posters, brochures, etc., and ensure their useful and appropriate distribution. Seek publicity from media. Consult official tourist bodies. Is any area at home or abroad likely to have special interest? Bear in mind that foreign tourists alone will not guarantee success; visits from within a country will form the basis of success and financial support. Consider advisability of allocation of block bookings to travel agents, coach operators, etc., and encouragement of package tours. Leaflet to contain information re hotels, restaurants, transport facilities, etc. Adopt symbol or emblem.
12 Consider advisability of attracting associated events.
13 Explore all means of recouping expenses including sale of brochures and programmes and advertising space, admission charges, bar and catering and souvenirs.
14 Consultation with police and motoring organisations.

This is a very comprehensive list and includes some requirements which might not be essential in the planning of small events.

Your tasks

1 Select a theme which would make an appropriate focus for a one-day festival to be held in your school or college.

You might choose to focus the festival on one of the following:

- a famous event from the past
- a local celebrity
- a particular art form like film or sculpture.

2 Use the planning sequence taken from the report on festivals to help you to decide on the size and membership of a planning committee for your festival.

Draw a diagram which indicates the responsibilities of the members of the planning committee and which also shows the lines of communication which will need to be established.

3 Set a suitable date for the festival. Use a calendar to draw up a planning schedule which gives a detailed indication of when consultation and action will be needed, and which shows who will be responsible for initiating it.

5.10 Fireworks at Alton Towers

Develops knowledge and understanding of the following element:

2 Present a plan for an event

Supports the development of the following core skills:

Communication level 3: Take part in discussions, Read and respond to written material and images (Task 1)

Communication level 3: Prepare written material (Task 2)

Among the many special events hosted by Alton Towers is a firework display. This requires thorough planning both because of the large numbers attending and also because of the nature of the event itself.

The first planning meeting for the event starts with a debrief of the previous year's event. A capacity is set and the latest regulations on Safe Practice for the Management of Outdoor Events, produced by the Health and Safety Executive, are carefully checked.

At this stage it is also important to establish the likely profitability of the event. Overheads are calculated, including stewarding and security costs, cleansing, extra lighting and signage for the event, mobile catering units, products and staffing for any merchandising activities, and additional radios to meet extra communication needs. Items such as cleaning will be particularly expensive since the Leisure Park will have to be open to the public the next day and cleaning teams will have to operate very late at night at then at first light the next day.

The fireworks display takes the form of a show with a series of scenes which first have to be designed. Once the content and length is agreed, accompanying music is chosen and timed. At this point three outside companies are contracted. A pyrotechnical company

Fireworks display at Alton Towers

plans and makes the fireworks, a lighting and laser company plans the visual effects and a third company plans the sound and public address systems. Eight weeks before the event a technical meeting is called in which all the elements of the show are drawn together. A technical rehearsal is held two days before the event to check the sound and lighting. One track on the eight-track recording system used is reserved as a cue track, which enables all lighting and laser effects to be cued automatically.

A budget is set for the display, taking account of the experience of previous years and of the number of nights on which the display is to take place. Some of the costs have to be estimated. The fireworks themselves tend to be a fixed cost but the lighting costs will depend on the amount of time they are actually being used.

A firework display of this size would normally require an Entertainments Licence, which is not granted automatically. The terms of such a licence have to be negotiated and stipulations are laid down about crowd size, noise, access and toilet facilities. The licensing authority, in this case Staffordshire, would need to be satisfied about a range of health and safety issues. These would include a check on physical structures, such as staging and barriers, and electrical and mechanical installations. The sound emitted by the PA system has to be measured at various points around the site. Assurances about the safety of food and drink supplies would be sought, including a restriction on any materials thought to be potentially dangerous, such as bottles. Alton Towers, given the expanse of water on the site, is also required to have a lifeboat and lifeguards available.

Once the planning is under way contracts are drawn up between Alton Towers and other participating companies. As well as stipulating fees, these contracts lay down conditions about the use of the site. They cover insurance issues in the event of cancellation, injury, loss or damage. They insist on compliance with regulations, including the protection of grass areas by the use of trackway covers.

As the event draws near final schedules are drawn up. These include a fit-up schedule which gives accurate timings for the delivery and installation of equipment. An event schedule, circulated to all participating employees, gives detailed timings of all activities during the event itself. In the interests of maintaining good public relations, a letter is sent out just before the event to all the residents of the local villages, giving them notice of the event and offering them free tickets.

Your tasks

Lazydaze Leisure Park, situated about 20 miles from the nearest town and without a regular public transport service, nevertheless attracts visitors well into the autumn. Most of them are attracted by the permanent fairground, the sizeable boating lake and an attractive natural arena, flanked on two sides by grandstands and frequently used for open air displays and concerts.

The managers of the Park decide to hold an early evening firework display at a weekend towards the end of the season. In order to secure good attendance, a special offer ticket is made widely available, combining a reduced rate entrance to the fairground with a ticket for the firework display. This is expected to increase the number of daytime visitors, particularly in the afternoon.

I   Study the map below and then discuss ideas for coping with the following issues and concerns which have been raised:

   a)   Equipment and materials will need to be brought in, and lighting and electrical work carried out, during the time when the Park is open to the public.

   b)   Some visitors will be inside the Park during the day with combined tickets; others will arrive during the late afternoon wanting tickets for the firework display only. The latter will have to be admitted to the Park as they can not be kept queuing on the main road.

Sketch map of Lazydaze Leisure Park

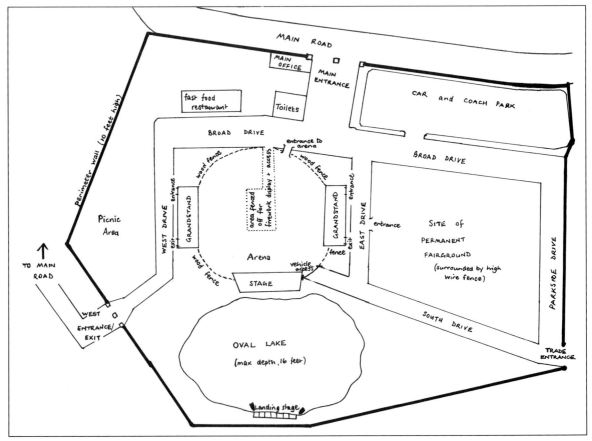

c) The car and coach park is unlikely to be able to accommodate all visitors if the numbers predicted actually turn up.

d) Crowds could build up causing dangerous congestion in two places: in East Drive where the entrance to the fairground faces the entrance to the grandstand and on Broad Drive between the entrance to the arena and the toilets and restaurant.

e) There is no segregation of cars and pedestrians in the area around the main entrance.

f) The Security Department has expressed concern about the adequacy of the fencing round the arena, though recognises that complete replacement may not be affordable in the short term. They are also concerned about the difficulty of patrolling the perimeter fence when staff will be needed elsewhere.

g) The siting of two additional mobile food outlets and a mobile toilet unit has still to be agreed.

h) The footpaths around Oval Lake are easily accessible from both West and South Drive, as is the landing stage where the small boats are moored.

2 Propose a suitable plan, with explanations, for each of the following event needs:

  a) a safe and rapid evacuation procedure

  b) a suitable site for a small medical unit, able to respond quickly to emergencies when the Park is at its most crowded

  c) a plan to enable the fire service to respond quickly in an emergency, taking note of the evacuation procedure described in (a).

Unit 6 Maintaining information services

6.1 Office technology and information handling

Develops knowledge and understanding of the following element:
I   Plan a management information service for a facility

Supports the development of the following core skills:
Information technology level 3: Set system options up, use and input data into storage
    systems (Tasks 1, 2)

Not many years ago you could walk into an office and find it full of files, paper, letters and index cards. Like other industries, tourism has benefited from the increasing use of electronic devices which enable information to be stored and communicated much more rapidly and efficiently.

Filing methods using paper or card systems take up increasing amounts of space as the quantity of paper grows. Computer databases will store vast amounts of information while taking up little space. Finding and altering files can be done in one operation. Information which previously might have taken hours of hunting through paper files to find can now be retrieved in seconds. Each record in a database file can be divided into fields, each of which gives a different kind of information such as name, address, sales record and so on. The information in the files can be ordered in different ways, for example either alphabetically, chronologically or on the basis of any field within the individual records. Totals and other calculations can be performed automatically. Records and information can be changed without having to rewrite the whole file.

Sending messages is very important in any kind of office operation. Using postal or despatch services can mean a wait of several days for information to arrive. There are a number of systems now available which enable messages to be sent electronically. Telex messages are sent by dialling the number of a company and, once connected, by typing a message. Copies of the message are produced by the printers at both ends of the communication. A code system is used to prove that the call went to the intended receiver. Teletext is an electronic mail service which works more quickly than telex. It can be operated through an electric typewriter or a computer. The text is prepared on a teletext terminal and can then be sent either to a single receiver or to several destinations by pressing the right buttons. Facsimile machines (often called fax machines) are used as a means of sending exact copies of documents via the telephone system. This is particularly useful where the document contains diagrams or illustrations, but its main advantage is that the receiver's copy is arriving at the same time as the sender is transmitting it – a much faster system than sending documents by post.

Most offices will have a range of sophisticated electronic equipment.

In the travel industry much communication is international. Satellite links have dramatically increased the speed at which messages can be transmitted across the world. Information is aimed from dish aerials at a satellite. The message is carried by a beam which bounces back off the satellite so that it can be picked up by a receiving aerial. In this way information can pass half way around the world in seconds.

Storing information is equally vital to the travel industry. Prestel is a system using ordinary telephone lines to connect computer-stored information with television sets or micro-computers. By dialling a page number, different types of information can be displayed. This might include information about travel timetables, entertainment listings, tax guides and company law. The system also enables messages to be exchanged, so it can be used to perform tasks like booking hotel rooms.

Larger companies find meetings essential but time-consuming, especially where the majority of those attending have to travel to the venue. However, letters and phone calls are often too impersonal a means of communication when decisions have to be reached which require negotiation and the establishment of trust between all participants. A system called Confravision now enables groups of people from different parts of the country to use a video display to see and talk to each other. This saves both time and expense.

Other applications of technology have enabled companies to cut the costs of sending and receiving information. Research suggests that only about one in four business telephone calls reaches the intended receiver first time. Systems can now be fitted to telephones which mean that if the person being called is engaged, their phone will accept an incoming call the moment they put the receiver down. The person using the telephone can be warned that the call is important by a bleep inserted into their conversation.

Your tasks

1 A school sports hall has up until now been used exclusively by school students.

The governors approve a plan to open its small weights and fitness room to the public on three nights of the week. Funds are allocated for the purchase of some new equipment. The Head of PE at the school is given a 6-month trial period to establish and manage the scheme.
List the types of information s/he would need to gather and store.

2 Devise a system for storing all the necessary information so that it would be secure but easily and quickly accessible when required.

6.2 Information and hotel management

Develops knowledge and understanding of the following element:

I   Plan a management information service for a facility

Supports the development of the following core skills:

Information technology level 3: Select and use formats for presenting information
    (Tasks 1, 2)

Information technology is playing an increasingly important role in the management of modern hotels. Larger hotels are likely to use computer-based management systems which may cover just the operations run from the front desk but which may integrate all the activities within the hotel which require information handling.

Most hotels will use computer software for their reservations and check-in requirements. This will also enable them to keep records of each guest's history and to generate statistical data to assist in managerial decisions about the hotel's future policies and practices.

Most of a large hotel's financial information will be generated by means of a computer. This has advantages for guests in that it can speed up the process of producing invoices and check-out information. Additional items such as drinks can be automatically transferred to the relevant bills and separately itemised.

Complete management systems will also make a number of other functions available. Communication between reception and housekeeping departments over morning calls, laundry, maintenance and special requests can be managed efficiently. The ordering of stock for restaurant and bar areas can be automated so that early advice of replacement requirements can be given. The risks of some of these stocks being stolen are also reduced. The system should also manage all the hotel's accounts, including sales, purchases and payroll records. It will enable management reports to be produced quickly in an appropriate format.

Most hotels use computer-based management systems.

An example of the way in which technology has speeded up the transfer of information in hotels is the system of billing telephone calls. Years ago a switchboard operator would have kept a record of all outgoing calls and written their cost by hand onto the relevant guest's bill. Calls are now likely to be recorded automatically and included as an item on a computer-generated bill.

Reservations in large hotels would once have been recorded on a display board, using some system of markers to represent occupied and unoccupied rooms. This was very time-consuming, especially since much of the information had to be entered by hand into record books.

Restaurant and housekeeping managers in large hotels need up-to-date information if they are to work efficiently. The Restaurant Manager needs to know how much stock to order and how much food to prepare. The Housekeeping Manager needs to know that a sufficient number of staff is available to clean and service all the rooms required. The number of guests and the number of rooms have to be counted each day. Many large hotels have a system whereby a housekeeper who has finished servicing an individual room simply keys a code into the telephone. This connects it automatically to a central computer system which then displays the fact that the room has been cleaned and serviced and is ready for use.

More modern hotel rooms offer an increasing amount of electronic gadgetry assisting the movement of information. These may include personal pagers, in-room answering machines and remote control television screens offering everything from messages to weather reports.

Your tasks

1 Discuss the reasons why a hotel might be interested in keeping a record of guest histories.
  Identify the information which it would be useful to include in such guest histories.

2 Use a computer to plan the layout, with suitable fields, for a single record to act as the model for a guest history database.

3 Outline the specific features of an automated stock control system which you think would significantly reduce the theft of stock from a hotel. Include an indication of the frequency and type of data you would expect the system to generate.

6.3 Management information systems in leisure attractions

Develops knowledge and understanding of the following element:

l   Plan a management information service for a facility

Supports the development of the following core skills:

Information technology level 3: Set system options up, use and input data into storage systems (Task 1)

Information technology level 3: Select and use formats for presenting information (Task 2)

Management information systems are simply methods of gathering data about a company's operations in a form which helps in making decisions, record-keeping, and improving efficiency. Even relatively small retail operations, for example, may use electronic point of sale equipment which generates information not just about volume of sales, but also about how different departments and different sales staff are performing.

Organisations handling large sums of money and employing many staff have particular need of good information systems. The payroll of such a company is an area where the data is complicated and where a manual system is time-consuming. In the past employees would have used time cards which were placed into a clocking machine when they began and ended work. The information from these cards would then have to be transcribed by hand onto record sheets to be delivered by hand to an accounts department.

Computerised time and attendance systems replace cards with swipe cards from whose magnetic tape information can be automatically recorded. General principles about salaries and wages entered into the system mean that the accuracy of financial calculations can be checked far more quickly. These systems also provide other kinds of information, especially useful to organisations based on more than one site. They can keep track of employees' movements. This may in turn indicate that some work, the maintenance of a particular piece of equipment for example, actually takes longer than they had expected.

Record keeping is an essential part of the work of a personnel department. Where several hundred employees are involved, the quantity of information needed is considerable. Apart from the legal requirements, most companies store data about their individual employees' working records. These may include appraisal documents, records of projects worked on, training records and any disciplinary matters in which they were involved. Even in a single area, that of holiday and sickness records, the company may wish to distinguish between a range of reasons for absence. Madame Tussaud's, for example, keeps records which enable each of the following reasons for absence to be separately identified: accident at work, accident elsewhere, discipline, death in the family, holiday, jury duty, leave of absence, absent on business, personal sickness, sickness in the family.

Leisure parks like Alton Towers use a computerised information system for their merchandising. Once an order for goods is placed it is manually typed into the system. When goods arrive at or are transferred from the warehouse to a retail unit on the site the information is similarly recorded. All goods are bar-coded so that electronic tills can record information about their price and sale. Overnight this information is downloaded to a central multi-user system. Access to this information is available at the warehouse and at the retail offices. Access to the information is limited by the use of passwords. This means that, dependent on the employee's function and seniority, they have access only to the information which they need in order to carry out their responsibilities.

The extent to which companies invest in computerised information systems is a matter of the relative costs and benefits. In addition to the cost of the hardware and software staff have to be employed to type in the necessary information for the system to function. Training and maintenance, often provided through contracts with suppliers of equipment, have to be paid for. The benefits are generally related to increased efficiency and time saving. In the case of merchandising they can also save money. A stock control system can reduce the amount of stock which needs to be held in store because accurate orders can be processed much closer to the time they are needed. This saves storage space and, more importantly, reduces outlay by delaying payment for bulk supplies.

Your tasks

Monty's Deck Chair Service, operating on the promenade at Sandcastle-on-Sea, employs four students each year from June to September. They all start work at 10 a.m., as long as the weather is good enough to encourage people to sit in deck chairs, and continue until 5 p.m. They receive £3 an hour but are not paid whenever the service is suspended because of the weather.

Barry, who has worked for Monty in previous years, is occasionally paid a flat £10 to deputise for Monty on his days off. On fine evenings, especially in July and August when a brass band plays in the Promenade Gardens, Monty sometimes keeps the chairs out for an extra two hours, paying £4 an hour for two of the students to work late.

Figure 1 below is an example of the manual records which Monty keeps for each individual. Figure 2 opposite shows how he summarises this information for himself and his four employees.

Name: *Len*	Week ending: *July 7th 1992*							Overtime	
	10–11	11–12	12–1	1–2	2–3	3–4	4–5	1	2
Monday	✓	✓	✓						
Tuesday	✓	✓	✓	✓	✓	✓	✓		
Wednesday		✓	✓	✓	✓	✓	✓	✓	✓
Thursday	✓	✓	✓	✓	✓				
Friday		✓	✓	✓					
Saturday	✓	✓	✓	✓	✓	✓	✓	✓	✓
Sunday				✓	✓	✓			

	HOURS TOTAL	*34*
	PAY DUE	*£102*
OVERTIME (*4* hours @ £4)		*£16*
	TOTAL	*£118*

Figure 1
Monty's records for individual employees

1 In what ways might Monty use his newly acquired home computer to improve his record-keeping?

Name Hrs/Overtime/Bonus	Monty		Baz			Jim		Doug		Lew	
	Hrs	OT	Hrs	OT	Bns	Hrs	OT	Hrs	OT	Hrs	OT
Week ending:											
Sunday July 7th	28	2	28	2	1	21	–	31	–	34	4
Sunday July 14th	35	2	28	2	1	24	2	32	–	28	2
Sunday July 21st	21	–	17	–	1	21	–	14	–	21	–
Sunday July 28th	28	2	38	4	2	28	–	32	2	35	2
Total Hours	112 + 6		111 + 8 + 5			94 + 2		109 + 2		118 + 8	
Total Pay	£360		£415			£290		£335		£386	

*Figure 2
Monty's summary of
employees' hours
worked*

2 The success of the Deck Chair Service leads Monty to buy up the nearby seafood stall, Ever so Shellfish Ltd. Local by-laws require the stall to close on Sundays and at 4 p.m. every other evening, and not to open before 10.30 a.m. in the morning. The former owners, Sid and Betty, agree to job share (doing exactly half the hours required each) for a rate of £3.50 an hour.

How can Monty reorganise his records system to accommodate both his businesses?

6.4 Restaurant management – documentation

Develops knowledge and understanding of the following element:

1 Plan a management information service for a facility

Supports the development of the following core skills:

Communication level 3: Read and respond to written material and images (Tasks 1, 2)
Information technology level 3: Set system options up, use and input data into
      storage systems (Task 3)

Managing a large restaurant involves handling a variety of important daily information. Reservations and their precise requirements need to be accurately recorded. Staffing arrangements and duties have to be drawn up and communicated. Stock control has to be efficiently managed, since daily demand will vary according to the menus offered and the number of bookings taken. A record of each day's business will have to be kept and if the restaurant is aiming for a high professional standard, this may include an evaluation of staff performance and notes of any comments received from customers.

In addition to this daily information, the restaurant manager will also need some information for reference purposes. This will include alphabetical lists of suppliers and companies with whom maintenance and repair contracts have been agreed. Information about all staff employed also needs to be held in a form which is easily accessible. This is particularly important in a business where people may have to be contacted at short notice.

Reference information for staff is also important in a restaurant. Individual employees

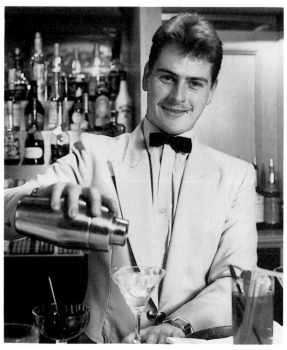

Efficient use of documentation can enable staff to give better, more relaxed service.

may need to look up details of food or beverages being served, for example the precise ingredients of a rarely asked for cocktail. The manager may need to refer to legal documents such as the Public Health Act in order to check the precise responsibilities which he or she has to carry out.

The layout of any documentation designed to carry restaurant information needs to make it both easy to use and easy to interpret. Seeing reservations listed chronologically may also help the restaurant to manage its busiest periods more successfully. It may sometimes prove possible for a restaurant to spread its business more evenly over a session which in turn enables staff to give better, more relaxed service. Such a list will certainly indicate when most business is being done and perhaps suggest how profits can be increased.

Your tasks

Study the two documents on the following pages – the Daily Management Analysis and the Daily Reservations – and answer the questions which follow.

1 The Daily Management Analysis

a) Why do you think it is necessary to write down the appointments and meetings which staff are due to attend?

b) Staff performance is measured on a scale of 1 to 4. What particular things would an assessor be looking for in deciding what score to record for 'waiting personality' and 'teamwork'?

c) Why do you think the margin notes include references to 'supervisory skill' and 'open management'?

d) What is an 'accumulative total' and why is there a need to record this for breakages and wastage?

e) Why do the margin notes suggest a connection between equipment maintenance and being short staffed?

f) Why are hygiene problems given top priority in a restaurant?

Daily Management Analysis

APPOINTMENTS ◆ MEETINGS	STAFF PERFORMANCE ✔		Lunch				Dinner				1 very good 2 good 3 average 4 below average	1 Don't forget, staff performance closely reflects supervisory skill.
Staff			1	2	3	4	1	2	3	4		
	Cleaners ◆ Kitchen porters											2 Do this exercise each session. Open management is demanding but worth it.
	Bar efficiency										3s or 4s	
	Bar personality										action needed?	
	Kitchen quality										Staff training!	
	Kitchen service											
	Waiting efficiency											
	Waiting personality											
	Teamwork											
	Booking spread											

Other

CUSTOMER COMMENTS ◆ REACTION

1 Record everything however minor.

2 Does anything point to a particular problem?

3 Do something about it today!

RUNNING LOW ◆ ORDER

BREAKAGES ◆ WASTAGE ◆ DETAILS AND REASONS

1 Put a price on it!

2 Keep an accumulative total and enter it in the box.

EQUIPMENT MAINTENANCE ◆ SAFETY

1 Keep your equipment regularly maintained.

2 Any problems, particularly electrical, deal with urgently. Don't end up short staffed.

HYGIENE PROBLEMS ◆ SPECIAL CLEANING

1 The new Public Health Act is not at all forgiving.

2 Everybody has a responsibility here. Wherever you see a problem record it.

3 Any problems indicated here are top priority.

GENERAL NOTES ◆ OTHER MESSAGES	TELEPHONE MESSAGES	
	For	From and number

Daily Reservations

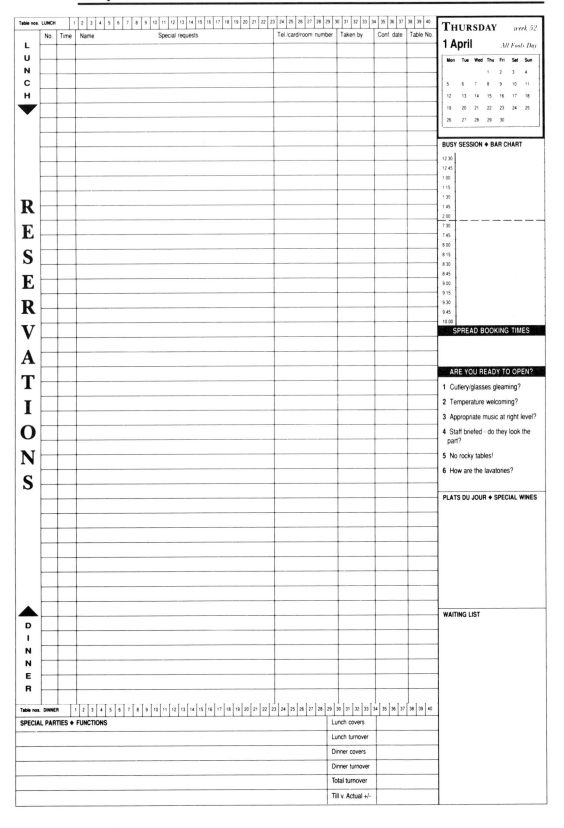

2 The Daily Reservations Page

a) Why do you think the table numbers are listed at the top and bottom of the document?

b) What do you think the Busy Session/Bar Chart space would be used for?

c) Can you suggest any other items to check before it was decided that a restaurant was ready to open?

d) What are lunch and dinner 'covers' and 'turnovers'?

e) What records are kept of the actual money paid by customers who have eaten in the restaurant?

f) What is a 'plat du jour' and why would the restaurant need to keep a record of what it was?

3 Neatley Court is a small hotel offering bed and breakfast terms only and containing two single rooms, six double rooms, and two family suites accommodating up to four people.

Decide what daily records the hotel would need to keep and plan a layout which you think would be both easy to use and easy to interpret.

6.5 Computer applications in the leisure industry

Develops knowledge and understanding of the following element:
2 Select and provide management information

Supports the development of the following core skills:
Communication level 3: Read and respond to written material and images
(Tasks 1 and 2)
Information technology level 3: Set system options up, use and input data into
storage systems (Task 3)

The first point where a visitor to a leisure centre would be likely to see a computer in use is at the reception desk. Its main function here would be to record bookings and issue tickets. Accurate information about availability can be provided instantly. Where membership schemes apply, keying in the visitor's number may also reveal other information, such as whether they are entitled to a rebate or whether their membership is due for renewal.

Where a number of centres are linked, for example within a single local authority, computers can be linked in a network which enables information to be shared. This would enable bookings to be taken at one centre for use at another. However the efficiency offered by computers is only likely to be sustained if staff are adequately trained to use the systems purchased by individual centres. The support offered by the company providing the computer and accompanying software will also be critical, especially in the first few

Computer software can devise an individual health and fitness programme.

months of using the system. Software systems are usually accompanied by working manuals, but these are not always easy to understand, particularly if the user has little experience of information technology.

Computer software can also be used to control access in leisure centres. Leisure centres often occupy large sites and remain open for long hours. They may have specific security problems, such as the expensive equipment kept in a health and fitness centre or the need for good crowd control at a sports ground. Magnetic swipe cards, issued to members, can be used both to give access to controlled areas while at the same time recording information about who uses particular facilities and with what regularity.

The growth of up-market health and fitness centres has prompted the development of a range of specific computer software. This performs a number of functions, mostly to do with analysing data about personal fitness, nutrition and food intake and personal exercise programmes. These programmes can analyse an individual fitness session and prescribe a health and fitness programme which takes account of the age, physique and life-style of the user. Software has also been developed which calculates the cost to fitness centre users in terms of the exact amount of use they make of it.

Membership schemes probably represent the most common type of computer use in leisure centres. Their advantage, apart from speed, is that membership records can be classified in a number of different ways which will help both accounting and marketing. In accounting terms such systems enable a quick check on turnover to be made. Rapid calculations of the levels of use during each period of the day and of the impact of offering discounts during off-peak periods can be made.

In setting up such a system it is important to think of all the probable uses to which it will be put. In a leisure centre the staff may change frequently, because of the long opening hours, and so the system chosen should not be excessively complicated. Members will not want to spend hours queuing either, so the systems will need to be capable of searching for information rapidly without the user having to key in a lot of instructions first. The speed at which the chosen system works will depend on the amount of data fed into it. A membership list requiring full details of 5 000 individuals will need a more powerful system than one required to keep only 100 records. It is also important that the system can generate reports in a format which is easy to interpret and useful to leisure managers.

Your tasks

A sample of four records has been extracted from the membership database of the Chalfield St Michael Golf Club.

On the following page there are four reports generated from data held about the four selected members.

1 Identify the main differences between the four reports.

2 Assuming that the whole membership database had been reported in these formats, what purpose, if any, might each of the reports have served?

3 Create your own database suitable for a school or college club membership, including fields for all the information you are likely to need.

Devise a method of generating different report formats, using selected data only, which would be appropriate for different specified purposes.

Chalfield St Michael Golf Club records

```
Record #: 1  Act: Y            Record #: 2  Act: Y
User: Johnson, Arthur          User: Millward, Marie
Membership no: 5643            Membership no: 6118
Date of renewal: 16/03/93      Date of renewal: 31/01/93

Record #: 4  Act: Y            Record #: 3  Act: Y
User: Merrington, Hannah       User: Suarez, Juan
Membership no: 25             Membership no: 2289
Date of renewal: 00/00/00      Date of renewal: 31/12/92
```

Record 1

```
        Membership no User              Date of birth
        ------------------------------------------------------
                 25 Merrington, Hannah     11/08/26
               2289 Suarez, Juan           13/09/56
               5643 Johnson, Arthur        18/10/40
               6118 Millward, Marie        07/07/48
```

Record 2

```
        User                  Gender Membership no
        Address
        Phone          Date of birth Status      Date of renewal
        ------------------------------------------------------------
        Johnson, Arthur          M          5643
        17 Hillside Crescent, Ruislip, Middlesex
        (089) 577-2132 18/10/40      full         16/03/93
        Millward, Marie          F          6118
        'Holly Tree House', Amersham, Bucks.
        (049) 465-5209 07/07/48      weekday      31/01/93
        Suarez, Juan             M          2289
        Stanley House, Firs Rd, Beaconsfield, Bucks.
        (049) 455-6810 13/09/56      weekday      31/12/92
        Merrington, Hannah       F          25
        6 St Stephen's Drive, Denham, Bucks.
        (089) 537-7726 11/08/26      life         00/00/00
```

Record 3

```
Date of renewal User
Address
Phone
---------------------------------------------------------------
00/00/00        Merrington, Hannah
6 St Stephen's Drive, Denham, Bucks.
(089) 537-7726
31/12/92        Suarez, Juan
Stanley House, Firs Rd, Beaconsfield, Bucks.
(049) 455-6810
31/01/93        Millward, Marie
'Holly Tree House', Amersham, Bucks.
(049) 465-5209
16/03/93          Johnson, Arthur
17 Hillside Crescent, Ruislip, Middlesex
(089) 577-2132
```

Record 4

6.6 Computerised reservations systems

Develops knowledge and understanding of the following element:

2   Select and provide management information

Supports the development of the following core skills:
Communication level 3: Take part in discussions (Task 1)
Communication level 3: Read and respond to written material and images (Task 2)

These systems, often referred to simply as CRS, provide central banks of information about scheduled airline bookings, car rental, hotel accommodation and the booking of leisure activities such as sport or the theatre. Travel agencies use computer terminals to gain access to this information and to make reservations for their customers.

In addition to the information needed to make bookings, many CRS systems enable travel agencies to build in client profiles. This means that the special requirements of individual travellers or companies can be fed into the system when a reservation is made. One company may wish to use only Business Class seats or it may have a policy about car hire or the kind of accommodation which staff of varying seniority are allowed to book. Individual travellers may have preferences for non-smoking areas or for window seats and this information can automatically be loaded by a single action. Most CRS systems also contain an instruction programme. This enables people working on their own to learn how to use the system by following a set of instructions and choices displayed on screen.

Galileo, probably the best known CRS in the United Kingdom, can book flights up to 331 days in advance. It can call up all available flights on a particular route, giving times, seat availability, fares, aircraft type and stopping points on the way. It can quote over 50 million fares and the airlines guarantee the prices stated as long as a ticket is purchased within seven days. Specific seats can be booked by referring to an airline seat map on the screen.

CRS systems get very heavy use at some times of the year. Many people in the UK book their holidays in January and so there are often times when a number of travel agents are seeking access to the same information. A queueing system can be used to manage incoming messages from airlines and hotels so that none is lost. Once a booking is made the CRS registers it immediately. This means it is always possible to give up-to-date answers about the availability of seats, rooms or cars for hire.

Package holidays can also be booked through a variety of computerised systems. The newest systems combine compact disk, video and personal computer so that the information about holidays can be accompanied by a video brochure of the hotel or resort. The visual display on the monitor can be changed by directly touching the screen with your fingertips. This means customers can make their own choice of resort and accommodation. They can specify the price they are willing to pay, include any special requirements such as a swimming pool and select from a number of choices offered to them. Though customers may require travel agency staff to advise them during this process, others will happily research the information for themselves, thus freeing staff to deal with other customers.

Technology has also enabled people to book holidays on the spot. Fewer staff are need to assist the booking process and holiday companies are able to deal with far more bookings than previously. For example, a large tour operator handled some two million bookings in 1987, dealing with over 100 000 on a peak day. This total was four times the number they had dealt with five years earlier.

Computerised Reservations Systems allow the rapid identification of unsold holidays. Tour operators are thus able to introduce special offers or promotions of specific destinations in an attempt to ensure that they don't end up with a lot of unsold holidays. The same process enables airlines to fill empty seats at the last minute.

CRS allow tour operators to make special offers or promotions.

The storage of information is important to travel companies. It enables them to send direct mail to previous customers. Computers can generate address labels and letters to named people at a considerably faster rate than anyone typing or writing them by hand.

In the future it may become possible to reserve holidays through a computer terminal in a shopping mall or a bank or even through an adapted television set in the home. Though this would make the booking of straightforward journeys much more convenient, many people would still go to a travel agent to book a holiday. They would want the advice and personal contact, in particular to boost their confidence in making a choice about a holiday, an expensive item from which they expect so much.

Your tasks

1 Would you prefer to receive information about holiday destinations you were contemplating visiting by means of a computerised display system or by discussing it with a travel agent? Why?

2 The table below shows a CRS on-screen display of flight availability from London Heathrow to John F Kennedy Airport in New York. Each flight is listed showing: a number, the departing airport, the arriving airport, the times of departure and arrival, seat availability, the airline, the flight number, the type of plane, the number of stopovers.

Study the table carefully and then answer the questions which follow it.

Flight availability from London Heathrow to John F Kennedy Airport, New York

28 SEP Tue 1200 LHR – JFK New York, NY, US. Use city codes LON/NYO for full airport availability

	Departure airport	Arrival airport	Time of departure	Time of arrival	Seat availability	Airline/flight number	Type of plane	Stopovers
1	LHR	JFK	0900	1200	FA DA YA BA MA	BA 101	74L	0
2	LHR	JFK	1030	0920	R9	BA 001	SSC	0
3	LHR	JFK	1055	1415	FA CA YA BA MA	UA 901	EQV	0
4	LHR	JFK	1100	1400	F9 J9 B9 K9 A9 Q9	BA 175	740	0
5	LHR	JFK	1200	1445	FA QA YA LA	AI 101	747	0
6	LHR	JFK	1200	1510	FA QA YA BA MA	AA 105	74L	0
7	LHR	JFK	1330	1650	FA CA YA BA MA	UA 903	EQV	0
8	LHR	JFK	1415	1720	F9 J9 S9 B9 A9 Q9	BA 177	740	0
9	LHR	JFK	1545	1815	FA YA	KU 101	747	0
10	LHR	JFK	1630	1910	JA YA BA KA LA	VS 003	747	0
11	LHR	JFK	1800	2130	FA CA YA BA MA	AA 107	767	0
12	LHR	JFK	1830	2130	F9 J9 S9 B9 K9 A9	BA 179	740	0
13	LHR	JFK	1900	1750	R9	BA 003	SSC	0
14	LHR	BOS	1500	1735	F9 J9 S9 B9 K9 A9	BA 215	740	0
15	BOS	JFK	1915	2030	YA BA MA QA VA	PA 4791	DH7	0

Key to seat availability: F = first class
C = club class
Y, B, M, etc. = other classes of seat
9 = more than 9 seats available.

a) What time does flight AI 101 arrive in New York?

b) What time does flight VS 003 depart from London?

c) How many flights do United Airlines run on a Tuesday?

d) Which is the only flight using a Boeing 767?

e) Which flights use Concorde?

f) If there were no aircraft code listed, how would you still be able to identify the Concorde flights?

g) What code should be used to call up the details of flights into all New York airports, including those other than JFK?

h) What reason can you suggest for the extra numeral in the flight code for the Boston–JFK flight (listed as 15); why is it listed at all?

6.7 Using research data for planning purposes

Develops knowledge and understanding of the following elements:

2 Select and provide management information

Supports the development of the following core skills:

Application of number level 3: Interpret and present mathematical data (Tasks 1, 2)

Few major business decisions are taken without research. This may be a matter of consulting existing reports or the results of past surveys or it may involve commissioning an organisation

Market research plays an important part in major business decisions.

specialising in research. The responsibility for leisure and tourism development within a geographical region is likely to rest with the local authority and they will have a particular need to know the probable impact of any new development.

Commissioning research into leisure and tourism impact starts with a brief. This will include the areas in which some data and conclusions are required. These might cover the effects of further leisure and tourism development on local employment patterns, on income generated, on other industries, on the local community, on the environment and local housing market. The brief could specify how much of the data should be quantitative, for example the number of visitors to the regions and proportionally where they come from, and how much should be qualitative, for example the perceptions of the area currently held by visitors.

The research organisation would propose methods of acquiring the necessary data. They could conduct a visitor survey at various locations throughout the region. In order to make sure that a balance was achieved it might be important to spread the surveys throughout the holiday season. Some data at particular locations might be affected by the fact that it was collected on the same day as a well publicised event. Card surveys could be used in different types of accommodation which agreed to circulate them to guests for completion and return. Telephone surveys might be used, particularly to establish the views of local residents and businesses. Research companies themselves will also draw on data to be found in existing reports. For example the National Census will provide useful regional information about employment and population.

The results of detailed research, particularly where it covers a whole region, is often lengthy. It may contain much statistical data, not all of it relevant to the individual users of the research. Sometimes an executive summary will be provided, giving simply an outline of the main findings and recommendations. Managers of individual leisure and tourism developments or proposed developments may need evidence from such research studies to assist their decision-making or to persuade others. Their success may depend on how effectively they select and interpret the data available.

Your tasks

Clayhampton Metropolitan Borough Council includes some attractive moors containing some picturesque villages. Clayhampton itself is an industrial town which developed largely as a result of the manufacture of textiles, but the numbers employed in this activity have declined rapidly in the last decade.

The Borough Council, aware of a steady rise in the number of visitors to the region and the potential economic benefits of this, commissioned some research into the impact of Tourism on the region. While some benefits to the region were already evident, residents of one or two of the smaller villages were becoming increasingly vociferous about the problems of congestion, noise and litter.

The seven tables which follow provide some quantitative data produced by the commissioned research. Use the data they provide to complete the task which follows.

Table 1 Characteristics of overnight stay visitors

		Number	%
Sex	Male	56	51
	Female	54	49
Age	Under 16	2	2
	16–25	6	6
	26–40	33	30
	41–60	44	40
	Over 60	14	13

Continued opposite

Table 1 continued

Work status			
	Full time	73	66
	Part time	17	15
	Full-time parent	2	2
	Retired	13	12
	Unemployed	2	2
	School/college	5	5
	Other	9	8
Occupation	Professional/managerial	43	39
	Administrative/clerical	20	18
	Skilled trade/craft	18	17
	Semi-/unskilled	8	7
	Trainee/student	3	3
	None	17	16

Among overnight stay visitors, 44% were found to be staying away from home for one or two nights, 38% for over two and up to seven nights, 9% for eight to fourteen nights and 2% for over 14 nights.

Table 2 Characteristics of day visitors

		Number	%
Sex	Male	142	53
	Female	126	47
Age	Under 16	3	1
	16–25	30	11
	26–40	91	34
	41–60	87	33
	Over 60	57	21
Work status	Full time	160	60
	Part time	25	9
	Full-time parent	10	24
	Retired	54	20
	Unemployed	2	1
	School/college	6	2
	Other	11	4
Occupation	Professional/managerial	92	34
	Administrative/clerical	52	19
	Skilled trade/craft	50	19
	Trainee/student	6	2
	Semi-/unskilled	31	12

Table 3 Number of adults in party

	Overnight visitors %	Day visitors %
One	9	13
Two	59	63
Three–six	25	15
Seven or more	5	8

Table 4 Means of travel

	Overnight visitors %	Day visitors %
Car (driver)	52	50
Car (passenger)	25	23
Bus (public)	6	9
Train	13	8
Coach/minibus	4	9
Other	1	2

Table 5 Activities and associated location

Location	Activity %	Overnight visitors %	Day visitors %	Total %
Activities undertaken on day of survey				
Countryside		66	43	55
	Walking	57	35	43
	Canals/water	15	13	13
	Other	4	10	8
Towns/villages		61	75	68
	Museums	23	16	18
	Theatre/concert	2	1	1
	Meal	27	20	22
	Shopping	30	31	31
	An event	19	28	18
Activities undertaken/to be undertaken on another day				
Countryside		40	2	
	Walking	26	2	
	Canals/water	13	0	
	Other	10	3	
Towns/villages		35	3	
	Museums	6	1	
	Theatre/concert	4	1	
	Meal	25	1	
	Shopping	20	1	
	An event	7	3	

Table 6 Average spending by visitors

	In Clayhampton	Elsewhere
(a) Day visitors not spending a night away from home		
	£	£
Fuel/travel	2.55	1.19
Food and drink	4.23	0.80
Leisure	3.60	0.33
Retail	1.56	0.93
Other	0.44	—

Continued on following page

Table 6 continued

(b)　Visitors on a day visit from accommodation outside Clayhampton

Fuel/travel	2.00	3.06
Food and drink	6.19	1.25
Leisure	3.86	0.31
Retail	0.37	0.93
Other	–	–

(c)　Overnight visitors

Accommodation	31.60	–
Fuel/travel	8.42	2.51
Food and drink	15.32	1.99
Leisure	3.36	0.36
Retail	5.97	1.92
Other	0	0.75

Table 7 Types of accommodation

	Number	%
Hotel	32	12
Guest house/B and B	59	22
Hostel	11	4
Self-catering	21	8
Caravan	32	12
Camping	13	5
Friends/relatives	94	35
Unsure	8	3

Your tasks

1　Mr A has a background in catering. He has sold his house in the South East, thus releasing some capital, and moved to the Clayhampton area to live with his aged mother. He intends to approach a local bank for a business loan to start up a catering business of some sort. He decides to use data from the Clayhampton Borough Council research to persuade the bank that his plan is realistic enough to have a good chance of success in this particular area.

Write the introduction to his proposal, selecting and interpreting data from the research.

2　Mrs B has been appointed to manage a new leisure and activity centre in the Clayhampton area. The site selected is on land formerly occupied by a now demolished canal-side warehouse. There are good hill walks, but none starting within a 5-mile radius of the site. Tennis courts and an open air pool will be constructed as long as the Borough Council can be convinced that visitors will pay sufficiently high admission charges eventually to recoup the costs. There is a strong tradition of local crafts, including dry-stone walling and weaving. Mrs B has been asked to submit a proposal to Clayhampton Metropolitan Borough Council suggesting the range of activities which would appeal to potential visitors and which would be most likely to keep the centre financially viable.

Write her report, using data from the Borough's own research to support her proposals.

6.8 Data protection

Develops knowledge and understanding of the following elements:

2 Select and provide management information

Supports the development of the following core skills:

Communication level 3: Take part in discussions (Task 1)

Information technology level 3: Set system options up, use and input data into storage systems (Task 2)

Information technology level 3: Select and use applications (Task 3)

Data about many aspects of our personal lives is held in computerised records. Anyone driving a licensed vehicle, or paying National Insurance contributions or holding credit cards will be aware that details like their name, address, income and health records may be held by organisations outside their personal control. Most people would not wish this information to be passed on, although the growing amount of unsolicited mail which most of us receive suggests that names and addresses are not regarded as confidential.

There are clearly strong reasons for keeping financial information secure, not least because of the need to protect individuals against fraud and theft. Yet even this issue can lead to conflict. Banks, for example, are legally obliged to inform the Inland Revenue of any interest paid to account holders, regardless of whether the individuals have declared such earnings on the income tax return form. Customers wishing to use credit cards to finance expensive items such as holidays find that the banks will indicate to the selling company any individual credit limit set.

While the release of certain financial information can be defended on legal or practical grounds, issues relating to personal records are more contentious. School, employment and medical records can all be held in computerised systems. Most people would agree that the individual has the right to privacy in areas such as their personal medical history. Yet individual employers might say that it would be important for them to know about certain medical conditions. School and employment records may consist of some objective data such as examination results or dates of employment and promotion. The recording of subjective information, such as another person's opinion of an individual's potential, is often extremely misleading. It generally fails to record the reasons for the judgement, cannot take into account the prejudices of the person offering the judgement and is likely to become outdated.

Personal records which are not frequently updated are also likely to provide false impressions. The security of the system being used to store the records is equally important. Backup copies of files have to be kept so that data which has been corrupted as a result of faults in the system can be quickly restored. Access to personal data should restrict the possibilities of any deliberate interference, alteration or unauthorised copying of information. There are two main ways of doing this. The first is to make physical access to the system difficult, either by using security guards or sophisticated locking systems which require personal identification to open them. The second method is to employ a system of passwords which allows different personnel access only to the data which they need to fulfil their particular functions.

In most European countries there is agreement on the broad principles to which all companies maintaining personal computerised records should adhere. They are required to:

- declare and/or register the use for which data is stored
- provide the data subject with a right of access to data concerning themselves
- maintain a prescribed minimum level of electronic and physical security in their computer system
- refuse to transmit personal data to any organisation that does not have similar controls over the use of data.

The Data Protection Act of 1984 outlined the conditions which would apply to UK organisations storing personal data. One of the first conditions to come into effect was one granting individuals the right to compensation if they had suffered damage or distress as a result of a failure to protect information held about them. From 1986 data users were required by law to register their activities with the Data Protection Registrar. In doing so they were required to explain the purpose of the data they were holding, the source from which it was obtained and any other organisations to whom they were planning to disclose this information.

Stages of the Act which came into force in 1987 gave courts the power to instruct data users to correct or erase records, where it had been demonstrated that these were inaccurate or untrue. Data users who failed to comply with a court's instructions could be removed from the Data Protection Register altogether, although this provision was regarded as a last resort. Individuals were granted the right to receive written copies of information held about them by any registered data user.

Underlying the Data Protection Act were eight statements of good practice:

1 The information to be contained in personal data shall be obtained, and personal data shall be processed, fairly and lawfully.

2 Personal data shall be held only for one or more specified and lawful purposes.

3 Personal data held for any purpose or purposes shall not be used or disclosed in any manner incompatible with that purpose or those purposes.

4 Personal data held for any purpose or purposes shall be adequate, relevant and and not excessive in relation to that purpose or those purposes.

5 Personal data shall be accurate and, where necessary, kept up to date.

6 Personal data held for any purpose or purposes shall not be kept longer than necessary for that purpose or those purposes.

7   A data subject shall be entitled:

    a) at reasonable intervals and without undue delay or expense:

       i) to be informed by any data user whether they hold personal data about that individual

       ii) to access to any such data

    b) where appropriate, to have such data corrected or erased.

8   Appropriate security measures shall be taken against unauthorised access to, or alteration, disclosure or destruction of personal data and against accidental loss or destruction of personal data.

Your tasks

1 Discuss the relative importance of the eight principles of the Data Protection Act. Then consider the implications for a large company of putting them into practice. What problems might they encounter and what solutions can you suggest?

2 The Data Protection Act does not cover files kept on paper in filing cabinets. Can you suggest any reasons for this? What difficulties might arise from an attempt to extend the Act to cover data stored in paper files?

3 A popular leisure park, primarily attracting families with young children, has 30 vacancies for staff to work there for the summer season only.

Advertisements are placed in the local press and applicants are asked to send a letter and CV.

Discuss the arguments for and against taking the following data into consideration when selecting successful applicants:
- school record
- previous employment record
- medical record
- credit status
- criminal record.

Unit 7 Working in teams

7.1 Organisation and management at Beaulieu

Develops knowledge and understanding of the following element:
1   Investigate how work teams operate

Supports the development of the following core skills:
Communication level 3: Take part in discussions, Read and respond to written
        material and images (Task 1)
Communication level 3: Read and respond to written material and images (Task 2)
Communication level 3: Take part in discussions (Task 3)

Beaulieu is the name most visitors use for a number of attractions to be found on the Montagu family estate in Hampshire. The range of these attractions and the different activities and facilities available at each one means that the organisation is a very complex one.

Beaulieu employs monorail drivers, accountants, artists, photographers, teachers, gardeners, chefs, vehicle engineers, carpenters, archivists, receptionists, shop assistants, woodmen and even a harbour master! The work of all these individuals has to be co-ordinated so that the attraction as a whole benefits.

Beaulieu employs a wide range of staff whose work needs to be well co-ordinated for the attraction to benefit.

Most staff are part of a departmental structure, covering areas such as Projects and Services, Public Relations, Personnel, Accounts, Shops, Events, Information Centre, Motor Museum and Engineering, Special Features, Catering, and Education and Interpretation.

The whole organisation trades under the name of Montagu Ventures Limited and most income received is paid to this company. All the historic structures on the Montagu Estate are leased to the company and the costs of repairing and restoring them is met from visitor income. In addition the Beaulieu Estate benefits by receiving rents for the properties leased to Montagu Ventures.

At least one outside organisation is involved in the provision of services at Beaulieu. All the catering outlets are run, through a concession arrangement, by J. Lyons & Co. In return for allowing them to run catering outlets and charge customers, Lyons pay a proportion of the income they receive to Montagu Ventures.

The National Motor Museum is an independent charity. It receives income from donations and sponsorship, as well as receiving a proportion of the gate receipts. The National Motor Museum Trust, which manages the Museum, provides a team of specialist staff able to run library, research and educational services related to the history of motoring. They liaise closely with Montagu Ventures Ltd personnel who are responsible for all the services providing the public with access to the Museum.

Another working team, called Beaulieu River Management, organises the letting of berths and the arrangement of mooring fees. They too pay a proportion of this income to the Beaulieu Estate as rental for the facilities leased. The rural areas of the estate are managed by the Countryside Education Trust. This organisation is itself a registered charity with a separate Board of Trustees but it works very closely with Beaulieu's Education Department.

A centralised Accounts Department serves all these organisations except for the catering concessionaires. Each manager is dependent on the Accounts Department to produce up-to-date information to help them to run their part of the business efficiently. Records are used to provide regular analyses of profit or loss. The department also ensures that all money is paid into the bank, that all bills are settled, and that all wages and salaries are paid on time !

A management structure diagram is available to show who each department reports to and where they fit in the organisation as a whole. Managers are appointed because they have skills in specific areas, so the Retail Manager will have a background in retail and will understand the problems faced by the departmental team. The Catering Manager, an employee of J. Lyons, and the Curator, employed by the National Motor Museum Trust, are not employees of Montagu Ventures Ltd. It is important, however, that they are part of the management team to enable good communication between their own and other departments.

Most management structures are hierarchical, with a Managing Director at the top and a number of management levels below them. The number of levels at Beaulieu is small which keeps managers closer to their working teams and reduces the chances of an 'us and them' atmosphere among the work force. For individual projects teams of managers with special skills may be asked to work together on the development of new ideas.

Your tasks

Use the Montagu Ventures Management Structure diagram on the next page to answer the following questions.

I Discuss which manager listed on the diagram would be responsible for each of the following tasks.

Montagu Ventures Management Structure

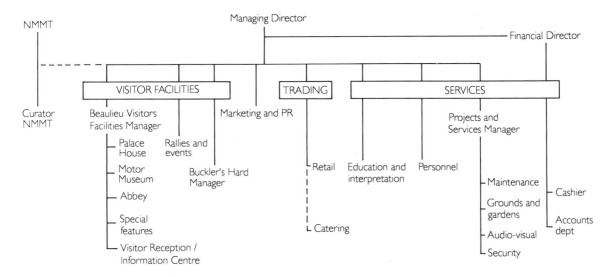

a) Drawing up plans for a future display interpreting the past history of the village of Beaulieu

b) Meeting the manager of a London coach company thinking of including Beaulieu in a new coach tour

c) Reviewing the shops' stock control system

d) Administering the Classics and Restoration Show, a one-day rally at Beaulieu for specialist car clubs

e) Delivering a training session on the subject of uniform and appearance to new staff.

2 Suggest suitable management teams for the development of the following new projects:

a) A summer season cruise from Buckler's Hard, on the Beaulieu estate, with an on-board evening meal and a live music performance included

b) The replacement of all the existing outdoor signage at Beaulieu and Buckler's Hard with newly designed signs

c) A charity event in which, for an agreed donation, participants accompany a celebrity in a veteran car drive from Beaulieu to Brighton

d) A *son-et-lumiere* show planned to illustrate almost 800 years in the history of Beaulieu Abbey

e) A mail order service offering video films featuring various aspects of motoring and motor racing history.

3 Discuss, in each case, which manager would be the most appropriate person to take overall long term responsibility for each of these projects if it was decided to approve and implement them.

7.2 Teamwork and motivation

Develops knowledge and understanding of the following element:
I   Investigate how work teams operate

Supports the development of the following core skills:
Communication level 3: Take part in discussions (Task 1)
Application of number level 3: Represent and tackle problems, Interpret and present
    mathematical data (Task 2)

An outsider's view of a successful company will often focus on individuals within it who carry the highest profile, perhaps the Chairman or the Managing Director. However the success is almost certainly dependent on good teamwork since there are very few companies where the managers do not spend a significant part of their time working with departmental or project groups.

To work effectively in a team people have to believe in the value and benefit of working in this way. It requires the company to create a sense that being part of a team increases rather than decreases the importance of individuals. The atmosphere has to be right too. For people to work successfully with others, there has to be trust and a respect for the skills and abilities of other people. Jealousy, negative criticism, and personal competitiveness need to be reduced if the team is to function well.

Not all teams, even if they accept the company ethos and philosophy, will behave in the same way. The nature of the tasks they are given, and the time and resources allowed, may affect their working relationships. If they have been told to do something they may react differently from the way they would respond if they had been consulted or taken part in the decision-making process. They are more likely to be positive if the group has clearly defined objectives, a known means of communicating its views and a belief that its recommendations will be acted on.

The combination of individuals in a team requires thought. Strong characters may clash; the more reticent may prove indecisive. The dynamics of the group may change as they get to know each other better, either gaining confidence in what they are doing or losing enthusiasm when problems are encountered. Even when a team is working together, it is important that the particular skills of individuals are identified and used to their full potential. For example, there is not much to be gained by rotating the responsibility for writing minutes of team meetings if two members of the team, who may be good at other things, prove quite unable to do it competently. Some individuals may be good planners; some may be good conversationalists, able to put others quickly at ease; some may be very practical in terms of converting ideas into working products and systems.

There are a number of factors which are essential for good teamwork. The size of the group should be appropriate to the task. A committee required to come up with a health and safety report in a small business might find it hard to produce clear conclusions if 20 people were on it. A full investigation into a major aircraft failure might fail to gather sufficient evidence if it depended on a team of two. The team needs clear objectives and a recognised means of making its conclusions known in the right quarters. The team can be helped to feel a sense of achievement if its work results in action or change. It may be that having a limited time frame will help to sustain momentum and keep the approaches of individuals to the task fresh.

Providing a team with its own working space is also important in motivating them. It shows what value is put on the work they are doing and increases their sense of identification with the task or project. Motivating the team is, however, likely to be more dependent on other factors such as the perceived importance of the work being done by the team. The level of interest shown by managers in individual tasks will indicate this. Sharing decisions and learning new skills and knowledge can also be important motivating factors. Sensitively handled, appraisal systems can be a valuable means of recognising individual contributions to a team and to a company as a whole.

Your tasks

1 The travel agency, Better Getaway Holidays, employs four regional sales teams based in Manchester (for the North), in Birmingham (for the Midlands), Bristol (for the West), and London (for the South).

   After a moderate year, the company wishes to increase its sales. Discuss which of the following methods you think would be most likely to motivate the regional sales teams most to improve their sales figures:

   a) Offer a free weekend holiday in Paris for the team making the most sales over a 6-month period

   b) Send each team a report of the sales performance of all the regional teams and ask them to account for the differences

   c) Provide a week's fresh training for all teams together in a Bournemouth hotel

   d) Offer the possibility of promotion to run new sales teams for Wales and Scotland to those with the best sales performance over a 6-month period

   e) Suggest that redundancies will be necessary if sales do not improve

   f) Stage a two-day conference for all sales teams to plan a strategy for improving future sales performance

   g) Arrange for the Managing Director to visit each team individually, to express appreciation for their past efforts, and to outline hopes for the company's future

   h) Offer a cash bonus to individual sales staff of £5 for every holiday sold.

2 Consider the sales figures for Better Getaway Holidays for 1991 and 1992 as shown in the table overleaf.

   Draw up a plan of action which would enable the company to use these figures to motivate rather than discourage the members of the four regional sales teams.

Better Getaway Holidays annual sales figures

	1990			1991		
	Number of holiday packages	Average value	Total sales	Number of holiday packages	Average value	Total sales
North Region	2000	300	600 000	2100	325	682 500
Midlands Region	1500	350	525 000	1600	325	520 000
West Region	1200	350	420 000	1400	350	490 000
South Region	3000	350	1 050 000	2000	350	700 000
Total	7700	337.50	2 595 000	7100	337.50	2 392 500

7.3 Leadership

Develops knowledge and understanding of the following element:

2   Work with others in teams

Supports the development of the following core skills:

Communication level 3: Take part in discussions (Tasks 1, 2, 3)

It is rare in any team exercise for each individual participant to make an identical contribution. Some are inevitably more influential than others. They may actually try to bully or dominate others. This may make them appear to be strong characters but does not make them good leaders since they are likely to overlook the potential of other group members.

The popular concept of leadership is often linked with famous figures from the past such as Churchill, Kennedy or Martin Luther King. These figures are generally remembered for their eloquence and forceful personalities. Yet there are many ways of getting people to do things apart from rhetoric and personal charisma. Leaders should aim to get people to do things because they want to, not because they are afraid or blinded by hero worship. Eisenhower described leadership as 'the art of getting someone else to do something you want done because he wants to do it.'

Any working team needs common goals. Each person in the team is likely to have different potential, in terms of their character and in terms of their skills and interests. They may all have some leadership qualities, such as being a good listener, having the ability to plan ahead, or communicating effectively with others. The art of leadership is that whoever assumes that role, whether permanently or just for a specific part of the task, is able to make the maximum use of the collective potential available. Simply dictating terms to the rest of the team is wasteful and is likely in the long run to demoralise the group.

There are many practical reasons why leaders should share responsibilities. People are more likely to complete tasks efficiently and with enthusiasm if they feel their ideas have been a valued factor in the process. They feel a sense of ownership of the task. Some tasks are in any case too time-consuming to be completed by leaders or managers and so they

Effective leadership means managers and staff looking together for ways to meet company objectives.

must depend on others. They have to delegate tasks and responsibilities appropriately, so that members of a team feel that they know what they are doing and that the responsibility given measures up to their experience and skills.

Leaders must be able to pass on their commitment to the task or organisation since, otherwise, perfectly able team members may refuse to recognise the importance or purpose of a particular project. The relationship between leaders and followers can be affected by a range of personal factors. Trust is essential and can only be gained if the leader acts with integrity towards others and is seen to set a good example. Depending on the team and the task this may require vision, tact, sympathy, encouragement, detailed planning, expert knowledge, good communication, an ability to demonstrate, a willingness to share the burden of work, or any combination of these.

Some people see leadership as simply exercising control. An example of this style has been light-heartedly characterised as the 'seagull style of management', where the boss is constantly hovering over people's shoulders and, when things go wrong, immediately drops the responsibility on them. However most recent studies of leadership have suggested that vision is the most important factor in achieving success. This involves identifying needs, developing ideas which can achieve them, communicating these to working teams, and sustaining a high level of motivation in the work force. It is a style which requires leaders to set an example to others, to encourage others to be active, and to look together for ways of improving what they do and how they do it. This obviously implies that if team members or employers are unable to meet their objectives, leaders will not be able to achieve theirs either.

The individual members of any team have different personalities. Effective leaders need to be able to make contact with individuals and gain their respect. They can't do this if they give instructions and then disappear! Personal contact shows they are interested and ensures they understand better all stages of the working process, as well as making individuals feel more important. Improving self-confidence and self-esteem within a team quickly raises morale and motivation. Insisting that team members know their place and do not compete for the limelight with managers often has the opposite effect. If a task is to be successfully completed, it should be done the best way. Good leaders do not insist that their way of doing things is always the only acceptable method of getting the job done.

There are other reasons for encouraging the development of leadership qualities. Most teams will require new leaders at some point in the future and it is important to identify those who will fulfil the role most effectively. Many individuals need an image of their future potential development. It helps to guide their ideas about what they are doing and to develop their individual strengths. It is not easy to motivate someone who feels that their role will remain unchanged indefinitely.

To sum up, good leadership is about changing attitudes and methods so that tasks can be completed in what all those working on them agree is the best way.

Your tasks

1 Divide into groups of four or five. Consider each of the following tasks in turn:

   a) Planning and publishing the schedule of activities for a newly-opened sports hall

   b) Organising a 'Tidy Up Our Village' campaign

   c) Designing and making an award for the restaurant in your region judged to offer the best welcome to customers

   d) Planning a sponsored event to raise funds for enhancing the leisure activities available in a local community centre

   e) Establishing a nature trail suitable for 8-13-year-olds.

   Discuss the roles and responsibilities you think members of the group would have to take on in order to complete each of these tasks.

   Consider what kind of leadership you think would be appropriate for a team intending to tackle each task.

   List the qualities needed and then appoint each member of the group as project leader for one of the above tasks.

2 Each member of the group should prepare an initial briefing for the others about the nature of the task they have agreed to lead and how they propose the group should approach it. They should then make a short presentation developing their ideas.

3 Each presentation should then be evaluated in terms of the leadership qualities which the group had earlier identified as being important to each specific task.

7.4 Conflict and co-operation at work

Develops knowledge and understanding of the following element:
2   Work with others in teams

Supports the development of the following core skills:
Communication level 3: Take part in discussions (Tasks 1 and 2)

Most people are fortunate enough to have friends. They may be people with shared interests, with similar personalities, of similar age, or with any combination of these factors.
Though they may disagree about individual issues, they each find likeable characteristics
in the other. Working teams may contain friends, but it is equally likely that they will contain individuals who are either indifferent to each other or, worse, experience a mutual
dislike.

Animosity or aggression is rarely constructive in a work situation. Personal dislikes
can easily lead to criticism and mistrust, both of which will contribute to an atmosphere in
which people find it difficult to work effectively. However, many personal dislikes are too
strong to change. It is the task of the manager or team leader to establish trust and respect
for each individual. This may be done through raising awareness of the rights and responsibilities of everyone involved in the work team.

The easiest atmosphere in which to work with someone you do not like is one where
the importance of achieving overall objectives is agreed and where standards of judging
individual contributions are consistently applied. Everybody should be accountable for
what they do and there should be no evident favouritism, especially where rewards or con-
cessions are concerned.

A number of factors may give rise to conflict within work teams. The pressures of the
job may be the most common one, for example where staff waiting at table in a busy

Staff serving in a restaurant may pass on pressure to serve quickly onto staff working in the kitchens.

restaurant are passing the pressure to be served quickly which they receive from customers onto staff working in the kitchens. All of us are subject to changes of mood. The consequences of a domestic row or a difficult journey to work can lead some personalities into conflict with the next human target – their colleagues at work. Some companies send managers and employees on training courses aimed at raised their levels of self-awareness and awareness of others in the belief that such training can reduce conflict.

Poor communication is a common cause of conflict at work. Tasks which are not explained clearly, messages which are indecipherable or not passed on at all, and documentation which is inaccurate create resentment, usually targeted at an individual perpetrator. The manner of spoken communication can also cause resentment, particularly if junior employees feel they are being patronised or criticised unreasonably.

Whatever precautions are taken, most companies will experience lack of co-operation from individuals or work teams from time to time. A team of waiters may feel that one of their number is too slow and is leaving them with more work to do. A museum guide may make it evident to visitors that they are less than enthusiastic about the collection. To solve these conflicts and ensure future co-operation someone has to confront them. The first task here is to identify accurately both who is responsible and the likely causes of conflict.

The task of resolving conflict usually lies with managers. If they decree solutions without consultation they are unlikely to remove the resentment. If they lose the respect and sympathy of those responsible it may be difficult to win them back in the future. In industries like leisure and tourism, which are so dependent on people, the answer to most conflicts and disputes should be personal. As a recent article addressed to leisure managers suggested, 'people's performance does nothing more nor less than reflect your expectation and the way that they are treated.'

Your tasks

1 a) List what you consider to be your own strengths and weaknesses.

   b) List six of your own general likes and dislikes about other people's behaviour.

   c) Discuss whether any of these could lead to conflict in a work situation and what the best way of resolving such conflict would be.

2 Your school/college has a small but valuable collection of paintings or manuscripts and decides to open these to public view. Personnel to implement this are to be drawn from your own student group.

   Three of the functions you will need to provide are teams of between 3 and 5 people to:
   ● design a brochure advertising the collection
   ● act as guides for visitors
   ● plan the financial management of the scheme.

   Discuss which individuals would make the best combinations for each of these three teams and why. Unless there are fewer than 9 of you, no person should appear in more than one team.

7.5 Games as teamwork training

Develops knowledge and understanding of the following element:
2   Work with others in teams

Supports the development of the following core skills:
Communication level 3: Take part in discussions (Tasks 1, 2, 3, 4, 5)

Learning to work with others is generally a gradual process. Many companies feel it involves skills which can be encouraged by a variety of training methods, including role plays, simulations and games. These activities have the advantage over training in a real work context in that they are controlled and short term. This means performances can be quickly analysed and key skills identified without interrupting normal daily work processes. The activities can be structured to focus on specific skills or qualities. They can require participants to adopt other roles than their usual working ones, making them more adaptable and more aware of the perceptions of others who work with them.

A typical training session aimed at building up teamwork skills might begin with an 'ice breaker' – a game intended to get participants talking to each other. An example might be that partners have to describe the best holiday they ever had to each other and then report back their partner's experience to the whole group. Stickers might be placed on the back of each participant, one set giving a range of dates, the other giving corresponding famous events which happened on those days. Finding the partner with the corresponding label establishes verbal contact in a context which is fun.

Communication is an essential part of good teamwork and there are many games designed to improve this. Most focus on the spoken word, perhaps largely because the majority of day-to-day work communication is likely to be oral. A common example is the game where one person has a note pad or flip chart and faces away from their partner. The partner is given a drawing or diagram and has to give instructions so that it can be drawn with reasonable accuracy. Two-way communication can be encouraged by allowing the 'artist' to ask questions. Pressure to work together more effectively can be introduced by the setting of a time limit, or by restricting answers to questions to 'yes' or 'no'.

Sometimes the purpose of the training may be as much about the way things are said as about what is said. Role plays, simulating real work situations, can meet this need, particularly with reasonably experienced employees. Some trainers will film or record these performances and then analyse them. While this may be appropriate for those with the confidence or seniority to handle it, it is likely to inhibit many people. Games where participants have to say given sentences or phrases in different ways, sometimes regardless of their meaning, are a gentler introduction. They can be asked to emphasize underlined words, or speak them with different feelings - sympathy, irritation, or amusement for example.

Setting a puzzle is a common method of getting a team to begin to work co-operatively. This can be a relatively simple exercise, such as assembling a number of irregular shapes so that they form a recognisable geometric figure or arranging a random series of words into the longest comprehensible sentence possible. An element of competition can both increase the fun and stimulate individuals to build on the ideas of others. A game which requires both co-operation and communication is called the Newspaper Race. Teams are given identical piles of randomly mixed newspaper sheets, each pile made up from the complete contents of five different newspapers. Each team sits in a line, in single file so that can only see the back of the person in front. The object of the game is for each team to reassemble the original five newspapers. Clearly good communication and organisation are essential!

Many teamwork games encourage the development of roles within the group. This would apply to the games which include an element of designing or building. A popular example requires each team to design and make make a full set of clothing for one individual using only newspaper and Sellotape. If all five members of a team work on design at the same time, or if they all watch one person sticking together a jacket, the value of being in a team may be shown up by the efforts of a group which plans its efforts jointly. Design and make exercises are a useful means of seeing whether different skills can be harnessed by a team. One individual may be very creative, another very dextrous, and a third good at planning an effective schedule.

Many companies use training to develop good teamwork among their staff.

Another category is the kind of game intended to build up the level of trust between working colleagues. Outward bound courses usually contain a strong element of this, encouraging a sense of physical reliance on both the individual and the team as a whole. On a simpler level is the game which requires members of a team to line up in two rows facing each other. Starting quite close to one another, a fresh egg is thrown in such a way that it can be caught by the person opposite without it breaking. The thrower retires to the back of the team and hence the distance thrown gradually increases. The team establishing the longest distance between thrower and successful catcher wins. Needless to say, best working clothes are rarely worn for this game!

Some games are intended to increase the sense of shared purpose in a team. Especially in leisure and tourism, the way customers perceive individual companies or attractions is affected by the attitude of the staff. Games aimed at developing a sense of company ethos may include writing acrostics based on the name of the company or attraction or on some words crucial to its success, such as *visitors*, *image* or *presentation*. Discussion of the ideas composed by the participants draws attention to the company's philosophy and what it hopes all its staff are striving for.

Your tasks

Working in different teams for each activity, take part in each of the following games, some of which will require some prior planning:

1 An ice breaker

Each participant receives a sticker, placed unseen on his or her back, on which the name of a city is written. The object of the game is for all participants to arrange themselves so that the names of the towns read in alphabetical order.

2 Did you hear the news today?

Select teams of 4 or 5 people. One member of each team goes out the room and listens to a prerecorded news item or reads a magazine feature article. Making sure that they cannot be overheard, they describe its contents to a second member of the team, who in turn passes it on to a third, and so on until it reaches the last member of the team. The accounts given by each final team member are compared and the factors accounting for the differences discussed.

3 It's the way you tell them!

Study a paragraph from a school or college text book until you are very familiar with its content. Take it in turns to read it out as if you were:
- handing out a reprimand at work
- reading a love story
- commentating on the final three furlongs of the Grand National
- doing the voice-over for a TV perfume commercial
- practising your DJ patter
- selling a second hand car
- soothing an irate customer
- taking part in a family argument.

4 Solve this

Draw this diagram on a flip chart.

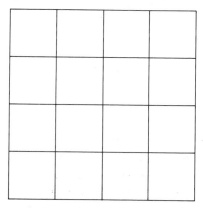

Each team should attempt to agree on how many squares they can see. They should nominate a team member to explain their answer to the other teams.

5 Trust me

Each team represents the news gathering team of a different and rival tabloid newspaper, each of which is keen to discredit the others. Unknown to the other groups, each team agrees that one of its members has a secret – entirely fictional but one they would wish to keep confidential. Each team member pairs off with a team member from another team in an attempt to gather a good story for his or her own newspaper. At the end of an agreed time the newspaper groups re-form and draft their planned front page stories. These are then compared to see to what extent confidentiality has been honoured.

7.6 Quality circles

Develops knowledge and understanding of the following element:

2   Work with others in teams

Supports the development of the following core skills:

Communication level 3: Take part in discussions (Tasks 1 and 2)

By 1982 there was a sufficient number of companies operating quality circles to justify the formation of a National Society. Quality circles consisted of small groups of employees, sometimes from different parts of a company and often with a range of responsibilities and experience, meeting to solve work-related problems.

The theory behind quality circles was that the involvement and participation of employees at all levels in investigating, analysing and solving work problems both improved the company's performance and helped to motivate individaul employees. Each quality circle programme could be set different objectives. These could be quite specific, asking them to do something like find a way of performing a function vital to the company operating more efficiently. They could also be more general, aiming to develop things like leadership, confidence or better communication.

Once a quality circle programme is in place, it will have an effect on the expectations of employees. It will not motivate if people feel the management is not committed to it or that its suggested solutions are not given serious consideration. Companies with a very hierarchical management structure may find it more difficult to implement such a system than those where the managers have more of an 'open door' policy.

This team approach to improving work practices does require commitment. Results are not going to appear overnight since all the groups will need time to gain confidence in each other and to plan their method of operating. Quality circles take place in company time and so participants are paid while the process is taking place. The system also requires some financial investment to cover training and training materials. This is necessary to ensure the whole-hearted support of the whole organisation for the system, by giving clear explanations of what the system means and what its implications are. Some training in teamwork, problem solving and in presentation skills will help to increase the chances of the programme's success.

Two other factors are crucial to the success of a quality circle system. It must be made clear that they are not simply an opportunity for discussion and that each circle has a goal to pursue. Interest in them will only be sustained if their work is recognised. Originators of solutions need to be ackowledged and due credit given. The company and its managers will need to find appropriate ways of expressing their appreciation if the increased motivation is to be long-term.

Most quality circle programmes are managed by either an individual facilitator or by a small committee. Their prime responsibility would be to maintain the links between individual circles and senior managers and to oversee the overall coherence of the programme. A facilitator may also have charge of training, of securing any funds needed, and of co-ordinating the programme of meetings.

Your tasks

'Brainstorming' is a technique used to get a group of people working together to suggest rapidly a large number of ideas. It works on the principle that participants will be stimulated by the suggestions and enthusiasms of others and that, although many of the ideas may have to be rejected, there will always be some good ideas remaining.

Read the suggestion about carrying out a brainstorming session.

Brainstorming
How do you start a brainstorm?

The first requirement is a flipchart on which to write down all the ideas. This should be positioned so that everyone can see what has been suggested. Next, the leader should explain exactly what it is the circle members need to consider, for example, 'What we are going to do now is make a list of as many work-related problems as possible.'

How do you conduct a brainstorming?

Brainstorming sessions work best in a relaxed atmosphere so that everyone feels free to contribute. There are four basic rules to remember when conducting a brainstorming session:

1 Each circle member should take it in turn to suggest an idea
2 Only one idea should be put forward per turn, even if the person thinks of more than one
3 If a person cannot think of anything, they simply say 'pass'
4 Most importantly, there should be no talking out of turn or criticism of other people's suggestions. No ideas should be made to look ridiculous. Remember that at this stage you are looking for a quantity of ideas and in many cases a wayout suggestion may spark off a good one from someone else.

Display the charts around the room so that all the ideas can be seen. Be as brief as possible in writing ideas on the flip chart, number them and leave a space on the left.

How do you sort out the ideas?

When everyone has run out of ideas, the next stage is to evaluate the list of suggestions. Each idea is discussed freely with the circle leader leading the discussion.

For example, if the circle have been brainstorming for problems, the leader should ask such questions as 'Is this an important problem?' 'Can we do something about this?', etc. If the circle think it is a good idea then it should be ringed. If it is a bad idea or if it appears more than once then it can be crossed out.

Other ideas might be important but outside the immediate control of that circle. In these cases suggestions should be starred.
Sometimes ideas may be linked with an arrow or a line.

How do you choose one idea from the list?

When you have gone through the list you will be left with a number of suggestions which have been circled. The next step is usually to choose just one of these. In most cases this is done by simply voting: 'Hands up those who want to tackle the problem', etc. At this stage the circle should be allowed to vote for as many as they like.

If, however at the end of this process you are left with a tie, then you can take a second vote, but this time with only one vote per person. The votes should be written down on the paper next to the appropriate ideas.

After voting arrange to collect data to confirm the choice. Sometimes it its not possible to decide by voting. In this case the circle may need to go out and gather some data to help them make the decision.

I Identify a number of problems relating to your GNVQ Leisure and Tourism course. These could include:
   ● how to increase the number of links between your school/college and the Leisure and Tourism industry
   ● how to build up a successful resource base for Leisure and Tourism studies
   ● how to reduce the cost of GNVQ Leisure and Tourism course-related visits.

   Select what you consider to be the two problems most in need of solutions.

   Divide into groups of between 4 and 6 people. Conduct a brainstorming session in which each group independently seeks solutions for the first problem selected.

2 Alter the composition of the groups. Conduct a second brainstorming session on the second problem identified.

7.7 Teamwork and presenting a good case

Develops knowledge and understanding of the following element:
2   Work with others in teams

Supports the development of the following core skills:
Communication level 3: Take part in discussions, Read and respond to written material
and images (Task I)
Communication level 3: Take part in discussions (Task 2)

Easthampton Museum has been in existence since 1878. The Padgett family began the collection by donating paintings and items gathered by Lord Padgett during his travels. A combination of further bequests and sensible purchasing policies by the Museum's Management Trust meant that, for a provincial museum, the collection was considered interesting enough by the 1950s to compare favourably with those in a number of much larger cities. Thereafter the level of funding gradually declined, however, so much so that currently the Museum finds itself in some financial difficulty.

Four groups have a particular interest in the Museum's future. They are:

- **The Museum Management Committee**: this small team is aware that the Museum is in urgent need of modernisation, both because some areas are looking increasingly dilapidated and because few young people are attracted. They have a strong desire to preserve the Museum's existing function as a place to exhibit artistic and cultural items. They are aware of the need to increase revenue if the Museum is to survive

- **The Friends of the Museum**: this small society has elected a committee to see that their interests are represented. The group contains people with a passion for art and history, including both leisure and academic interests. They are very concerned about what they feel is the steady erosion of local leisure services

- **Kind Arts plc**: aware of the Museum's financial difficulties, this company is preparing to submit a plan to convert the Museum into a mixed arts centre which will reduce the exhibition space and replace some of it with a cinema, a small theatre and an underground bowling alley. They have appointed a small project team to ensure that their scheme is considered alongside any other proposals for the Museum's future

- **Easthampton Borough Council**: the small team in the Leisure and Recreation Department is aware of recent public criticism of local leisure facilities. They have no funds available for any major development work, but they are seeking ways of raising the profile of the town in the hope of attracting more outside visitors. However the Council itself reveals a considerable division of opinion about the kind of image the town should seek to develop. Some are strongly for maintaining its traditional historical associations; others argue that it is failing to keep pace with the modern world.

The museum's three best known exhibits have, not surprisingly, been the focus of much recent speculation. A brief description follows of each one.

The Kumbet Vases: brought from Turkey in 1816 by Sir George Devonshire. Two matching marble vases depicting figures. The Turkish government claims they are part of their heritage and should be returned. A New York private collector has offered £3 million for them.

Nightmare: a painting by the abstract American artist, Elmer Lewis, donated in 1970 by Lady Padgett. A 15-foot square black canvas half-covered in red hand prints. The painting was described by one critic as resembling 'the product of a huge, unimaginative class of primary school children.' A major art dealer has valued it at £250 000.

The Kratzburg Fragment: an Anglo-Saxon manuscript, part of a much longer account of eighth-century life in North Germany. In a very fragile condition and no longer easy to read. However, because it is a unique record, regarded as priceless.

A discussion on local television, watched by representatives of each of the four groups already mentioned, raises six possible courses of action, though arguments are raised for and against each of them.

Each of the six proposals is followed by some of comments made about them:

1 'We should offer to sell one of the vases to New York for £1.5 million and return the other to the Turkish government.'

a) '...the vases were made as a pair and should always be exhibited as a pair. Separating them would be artistic vandalism...'

b) '...neither New York nor Turkey would be satisfied by this offer...'

c) '...the Turks would regard it as an insult to be offered half of what they regard as theirs in the first place...'

d) '...selling to a New York private collector would mean that the general public would no longer be able to admire one of the vases...'

2 'We should charge visitors an extra entrance fee of £2 to view a new modern art section, which would include *Nightmare'*.

a) '...museums should be for everyone, not just for those who can afford to pay...'

b) '...we should try to educate visitors to appreciate modern art, and not set it apart as if it were something different and difficult to understand...'

c) '...visitors would complain that they were being exploited...'

3 'We should advertise The Kratzburg Fragment for sale in American art collecting magazines for a price to be negotiated.'

a) '...it is a valuable piece of European history, and does not belong in America...'

b) '...it could pass into the hands of someone who does not know how to conserve it successfully...'

c) '...we could gain the reputation of being more interested in profit than in having unique artefacts in our collection...'

d) '...there's not much point in renovating the building if there's nothing of outstanding interest on display inside them...'

4 'We should offer to sell The Kumbet Vases to the Turkish government for £3 million.'

a) '...the Turkish people are not wealthy enough to meet that asking price...'

b) '...the vases rightfully belong to Turkey, having been sold previously by rulers who ignored the importance of heritage to their people...'

c) '...putting them up for auction could successfully raise a higher bid than £3 million...'

5 'We should offer to exchange the *Nightmare* painting for a more traditional picture, for example an oil painting of an English landscape.'

a) '...I can't think of anyone who would be willing to make such an exchange...'

b) '...we already have oil paintings of English landscapes in our collection...'

c) '...it is our responsibility as a museum to cater for a variety of interests, including minority tastes...'

6 'We should remove The Kratzberg Fragment to the safety of a vault away from public view, where it can be more effectively preserved.'

a) '...there is no point in keeping it if no-one is going to see it...'

b) '...we can't afford to have such a valuable asset serving no active purpose in the museum...'

c) '...though preservation techniques may extend its life, it can't last for ever...'

Your tasks

I Divide into 4 teams, representing:
- The Museum Management Committee
- The Friends of Easthampton Museum
- Kind Arts plc (project team)
- Easthampton Borough Council (leisure and recreation).

Discuss your reactions to the proposals and comments which resulted from the television programme.

Reach an agreement about which single proposal your group would give its full support to and prepare a short press release expressing your views.

2 Each group should now meet with each of the other groups in turn and attempt to establish the following:
- their main areas of agreement
- their main areas of disagreement
- issues over which they think a compromise might be reached.

7.8 Staff appraisal

Develops knowledge and understanding of the following element:

3 Evaluate team performance

Supports the development of the following core skills:
Communication level 3: Prepare written material (Tasks 1 and 2)

Evaluating the performance of individuals and teams at work can be carried out in a number of ways. Sometimes quantitative methods may be used. For example, the performance of a sales team can be measured in terms of the number and value of the sales they make. Personnel answering telephone enquiries can be assessed in terms of the number of calls they respond to and the average length of each call. Chefs can be assessed in terms of the time it takes to prepare a number of set menus.

Evaluating individual and team performance in a restaurant

Some work activities are difficult to assess in these terms, for example the quality of service in a restaurant or the effectiveness of the commentary given by a museum guide. Customer surveys may give some insight into the quality of service being provided, but many companies use a staff appraisal system to review the duties of individual employees and to see how effectively they are working with others. The system is used to judge how well each employee is performing and to identify their strengths and weaknesses. The process is not intended to focus on negative criticism, except where it is clearly deserved. The aim is to talk through each employee's current and potential contribution and to establish some future goals. This helps the company both in using each individual's potential and in matching them to work areas and work teams where they will flourish.

Appraisal is generally carried out by means of an interview between the employee and their supervisor or head of department. Often a standard form is used, listing a number of questions for the head of department to answer about the employee's work performance. It will draw attention to accomplishments, difficulties and ability to work with others. Judgement about the individual's attitudes is usually asked for, including their knowledge of their duties and of company rules and regulations and of their response to company initiatives. The process usually involves the employee working with the supervisor to agree the levels of performance they have achieved in various aspects of the job during the appraisal period. They will also agree future objectives.

There is a risk that this system will make employees feel as if they are being treated like children. To try and avoid giving the impression that appraisal is like an examination in which failure is unforgivable, many companies also use an employer appraisal form. This gives employees the opportunity to say whether their duties have been clearly explained to them and whether they think they are ideally suited to the tasks they are performing or the teams they are working with. It gives the company the chance to find out the factors which most encourage and most discourage their work force. It is often a means of identifying problems and obstacles which have not previously come to light. It can also give indications of where more experience or training would increase effectiveness. In some firms appraisal is used as a means of assessing suitability for promotion or as a means of deciding the rate of annual salary increase.

In jobs where some kind of management function is involved a job description is likely to have been provided at the time of appointment. These are valuable in appraisal since they provide criteria against which to measure performance. They will also in time show which areas of the company's business are changing and so demanding more or less staff time spent on them.

Your tasks

I List the different skills and qualities which you think ought to be regularly appraised in the following jobs:
- a museum guide
- a judo coach
- a pastry chef
- a coach driver
- a hotel receptionist.

2 Select one person currently employed in one of these five occupations. Use appropriate research methods to establish which other personnel they are required to work with.

Suggest an appraisal system designed to evaluate how well the personnel you have identified work as a team.

Unit 8 Evaluating the performance of facilities

8.1 Beaulieu: organisational objectives

Develops knowledge and understanding of the following element:
1   Investigate the organisational objectives of facilities

Supports the development of the following core skills:
Application of number level 3: Gather and process data (Task 1)
Communication level 3: Prepare written material (Task 2)

Since Beaulieu is made up of a number of different attractions, it has a need both for broad objectives, applicable to the whole organisation, and for more specific objectives which relate to the individual sites.

The overriding objective of the whole organisation is to ensure its continued existence and to enhance the facilities and services which it provides. This means working to preserve the beauty of the area, making sure that it continues to integrate well with the New Forest which surrounds it. Because Beaulieu has a long history as a family-owned estate there is a wish to preserve this status while at the same time making appropriate areas of the Estate accessible for public enjoyment.

Montagu Ventures is the company within the Beaulieu organisation which is responsible for the development and management of leisure and tourist services. This means that its objectives are both to exploit the commercial potential of the attraction while at the same time ensuring that this does not harm the physical environment. The company's objectives in managing the individual attractions are to ensure that they are both accessible and also capable of providing an enjoyable experience for visitors. In doing this they have to be aware of the potential conflicts which may arise, particularly in the more sensitive environments on the estate such as the riverside.

Exploiting the commercial potential requires the company to seek to attract as many visitors to Beaulieu without harming either the physical environment or the enjoyment of visitors. It also involves successfully managing the income which is generated. Montagu Ventures is not backed by a group of shareholders who expect annual profits from its activities. The value of this is that the organisation rates highly its purpose of restoring and conserving heritage buildings and landscape within the estate. Shareholders seeking annual dividends would put pressure on the organisation to spend less money on such improvements. Clearly the company also aims to utilise some of its income to improve the services and facilities available to visitors.

The motor car collection at Beaulieu is the responsibility of a charity called the National Motor Museum Trust. Their main objective is quite specific: to safeguard the future of the collection. This involves finding and purchasing new exhibits, restoring and

The National Motor Museum Trust aims to safeguard the future of the collection at Beaulieu.

conserving vehicles of historic interest, and researching background detail relevant to the Motor Museum as a whole. Though this might appear to be more an academic than a commercial objective, it is important to the commercial operation in that it enhances the quality of the visitor experience, by providing good public information.

The Beaulieu River Management Company has objectives which appear on the surface to be primarily environmental. The Beaulieu River is a navigable waterway and the company ensures that it continues to be so. It manages the movement and mooring of yachts so the visual appearance of the river estuary does not lose its appeal as a result of overcrowding. Anglers use the river in search of fish and shellfish and the Company ensures that this recreational use can continue by maintaining sufficient stocks of fish. Management of the parts of the Estate adjacent to the river is also the responsibility of the Company which seeks to ensure that this environment is kept clean and attractive.

Your tasks

1 Make a visit to a leisure or tourism facility close to where you live. Gather as much information as you can about the facility. Free leaflets may be available. Signs and notices may contain important information which you should note.

Establish how many different areas are open to the public and what is available in each of these.

2 Establish to which of the following sectors the managers of the facility belong:
- the public sector
- the private secor
- the voluntary sector.

Write objectives which might be created for the facility in the event of its being taken over by an organisation from a different sector to the one currently managing it.

You should include both broad objectives applying to the facility as a whole and specific objectives which apply to individual areas within it.

8.2 Visitor attractions: a national code of practice

Develops knowledge and understanding of the following element:
2 Plan the evaluation of a facility's performance

Supports the development of the following core skills:
Application of number level 3: Gather and process data (Tasks 1, 2, 3)
Communication level 3: Prepare written material (Task 4)

One difficulty in evaluating the performance of one tourism facility as opposed to that of another is the lack of agreed standards by which to judge them. In an effort to remedy this the English Tourist Board's Visitor Attractions Advisory Committee has drawn up a National Code of Practice. The purpose of the standards described in this code is both to safeguard the interests of the public and to reassure the tourist boards of the quality of the attractions they are including in regional and national promotions.

The Code begins by defining a visitor attraction in the following way:

A permanently established excursion destination, a primary purpose of which is to allow public access for entertainment, interest or education; rather than being a primary retail outlet or a venue for a sporting, theatrical, or film performances. It must be open to the public, without prior booking, for published periods each year, and should be capable of attracting day visitors or tourists, as well as local residents.

Attractions which conform to this definition can register their agreement to observe the Code and their performance against its standards are then monitored by the relevant regional tourist board. Attractions which do not register are not included in promotions and publications produced by the English Tourist Board. Registration entitles individual attractions both to display a certificate indicating the standards they are observing and to use a logo indicating that they participate in the scheme.

The National Code of Practice places an obligation on owners and managers of visitor attractions to fulfil requirements in seven areas. The first relates to the quality of information provided about the attraction. The code stipulates that it should be accurate and comprehensive. A particular concern relates to any specific conditions of entry. Potential visitors should know in advance if appointments are required or if children are not admitted. If parts of the attraction would be physically inaccessible to the very old or the very young, this should be made clear. Information about the site should not mislead. For example it should be clear which parts of the attraction allow free admission and which incur an entry charge. Publicity material should include clear directions about how to get to and from the attraction.

The second clause in the Code relates to entry charges. These should be clearly displayed at all entrances and should not disguise additional charges. It would not be realistic to list all the prices of food outlets and individual facilities at the entrance to large attractions, but the Code requires an acknowledgement at the entrance of the principle that such charges are made. Special charges agreed with visiting parties should be confirmed in writing so that the group leaders can bring written evidence of these agreed rates with them on the day of their visit.

The standards of customer care are highlighted by a requirement to ensure the safety, comfort and service of customers. Attractions must be clean. They must display adequate safety information and ensure that visitors receive good guidance. Equipment and facilities have to be maintained to a high standard, as well as being checked to see that they are fit for the purpose for which they are being used.

On-site facilities will vary according to the size of the attraction. The Code makes reference to toilets, coach and car parking and catering arrangements. These should, as far as possible, meet the likely demand. Signing should make them easy to find and, where these facilities are not available, publicity material should indicate this.

The Code looks for a willingness on the part of attractions to provide access for all people, whatever their particular needs. It is perhaps the one standard where evaluation requires a degree of common sense. It is very difficult, for example, for the owners of underground cave systems or owners of some historic buildings to provide complete access for wheelchair users.

The National Code of Practice looks for a willingness to provide access for all people, whatever their needs.

Any enquiries or complaints which are received should be dealt with quickly and courteously, regardless of whether they are spoken or written. If visitors do complain, the cause of their grievance should be properly investigated and where it is found to be reasonable they should be informed about what corrective action has been taken.

The final clause in the Code requires owners and managers to provide public liability insurance or, in Government owned properties, a comparable arrangement. Attractions should also abide by all other statutory regulations which apply to them. These might relate to such things as planning or health and safety.

Any registered attraction which is found not to be conforming with these seven requirements is first notified by the English Tourist Board. If the failure is not put right the attraction is withdrawn from the register and hence from any publicity or promotions of the national or regional tourist boards. Owners and managers who feel the original notification to be unjust, can submit evidence to an Appeals Panel which will give a final decision on the basis of the evidence and sometimes on a visit to the attraction.

Your tasks

1 Draw up a questionnaire which could be used as a guide by inspectors appointed by a regional tourist board to judge how effectively a visitor attraction was achieving the standards described in the Visitor Attraction National Code of Practice.

2 Make a tour of a visitor attraction in your own region and complete your questionnaire on the basis of what you observe there.

3 How many of the seven standards could be used in the following, each of which was excluded from the ETB's definition of visitor attractions:
- a travelling fairground
- an enclosed shopping mall
- an athletics stadium
- a cinema?

4 List other clauses which you think would need to be incorporated into a Code of Practice designed to assist in the evaluation of each of the four examples given in task 3.

8.3 Company quality assessment schemes

Develops knowledge and understanding of the following element:
2   Plan the evaluation of a facility's performance

Supports the development of the following core skills:
Application of number level 3: Interpret and present mathematical data (Task 1)
Communication level 3: Prepare written material (Task 2)

Successful leisure and tourism companies usually aim both to retain their existing markets and to secure new ones. A major factor in achieving this is to guarantee the quality of the product or service being offered. In the past evaluation of business quality was often done internally and so gave little indication of the company's performance in relation to its competitors. The British Standards Institute Quality Assurance scheme offers industry the chance to have its products and quality systems assessed independently. Achieving BSI certification is an indication to customers that certain agreed quality standards have been met.

The BSI scheme which measures the overall quality standard of companies is known as BS 5750. It involves a team of assessors who first look at the quality system in operation already. They inspect all the documentation which sets out the quality standards and how they are achieved in the organisation being assessed. Companies which consistently produce goods to national standards can be licensed by BSI to use the BSI Kitemark on them, indicating their quality to potential purchasers. Service industries can use individual schemes to check the quality of aspects of their operations. For example the Call Routing Apparatus Maintenance scheme ensures that all equipment connected to the national telephone network is properly maintained.

The general quality standards which make up BS 5750 can be applied to individual sectors of industry. A process of consultation results in the drawing up of Quality Assessment Guides which are used in applying BS 5750 to the particular process or service under consideration. Leisure and tourism companies seeking this kind of quality certification would need this kind of consultation, not least because their products are far less tangible than those of a manufacturing company.

The areas which would come under scrutiny include the management of the company. Staff held responsible for quality standards should be seen to have the power to make improvements. The means by which they check efficiency and good service should be well defined and understood by all employees. Communication of the company's quality standards is generally initiated through induction training and supported by means of manuals relevant to the different departments and operations within the organisation. American Express, for example, provides a pack for all its business and retail travel centres, setting the standards of customer service which the company expects. The standards cover telephones, reservations, documentation, customer service and appearance. Some of these standards, for example the time from receipt of a ticket to processing it, are measured on a weekly basis and the results are aggregated to give an indication of performance across all American Express travel centres.

The quality of documentation within a company can be a measure of its efficiency. It affects both its internal communication and awareness, as well as the impression it creates outside. Good records generally mean fewer mistakes and time saved by needless duplication. Leisure and tourism companies often buy in services from other companies, such as caterers, designers or public relations specialists. Setting criteria for the suppliers of these services and setting up a system to monitor the quality of what they contribute should also form part of any quality assessment.

Maintaining quality in adverse circumstances can be a major test for any company. Good organisations try not to resort to crisis management. They attempt to plan for contingencies so that, for example, in the event of the absence of staff with specific responsibilities others are equipped to deputise without significantly reducing the effectiveness of what is being done. Where things do go wrong there should be an agreed corrective process. For some problems this will require a full investigation and a means of communicating effectively what preventative measures have been taken as a result.

Quality assessment, particularly in an organisation like a leisure centre, should also include a review of how relevant laws and regulations are made known and implemented. Safety issues relating to the handling of materials, the use of equipment and first aid training will have special significance in some leisure and tourism contexts. Training and regular checks are necessary to ensure that awareness of these issues and all others relating to quality is continuous.

Your tasks

1 A large travel agency branch office employing six travel counsellors decides to monitor its telephone calls from customers. The manager selects a random half hour each week when all incoming calls are checked. The following information is noted: how long it took to answer the call; how long the call lasted; how many calls were lost.

Discuss how useful you think the data which was gathered as a result of this monitoring would be in judging the quality of service being offered by the agency.

2 Collect a number of examples of items sold as souvenirs at tourist attractions. Draw up a plan which would enable the makers to evaluate the quality of their products.

8.4 A new airport – the environmental impact

Develops knowledge and understanding of the following element:
3   Evaluate the performance of a facility

Supports the development of the following core skills:
Communication level 3: Take part in discussions, Read and respond to written material and images (Task 1)
Communication level 3: Prepare written material (Task 2)

Travel to many parts of the world has been revolutionised by the building of new airports. As facilities, airports tend to be measured in terms of the numbers of passengers who use them and, to a lesser extent, on the quality of the facilities available within them. It is less common to assess them in terms of their impact on the local environment and on the local people. Many of the larger modern airports evolved from small airfields and so were not originally planned with any notion of the volume of air traffic they now receive. In many cases their own growth stimulated an increase in the number of employees seeking homes in the vicinity, so that the surrounding areas are far more built up than could originally have been anticipated.

New airports have fewer excuses for not evaluating their likely environmental impact thoroughly. However, the economic prosperity of the country in which they are sited will influence the extent to which their designers build in features to protect the environment.

Noise is perhaps the most obvious example of an airport's impact. In many countries legislation will control the maximum noise levels permissable. Aircraft engine noise is particularly loud during take-off, initial climb and during the deceleration which takes place after landing. Longer runways could obviate the need for braking by using the noisy process of reversing the thrust of the engines. Aircraft engines are much quieter than they used to be but at times when the undercarriage and wheels are lowered turbulence increases the normal noise level. Some airports attempt to discourage older, louder types of jet aeroplane by charging them higher landing fees or requiring them to obtain special permission in order to land. All aircraft are divided into noise level categories which helps in monitoring the amount of noise at individual airports. Greater engine thrust means that modern jets can climb more steeply, thus reducing the noise at ground level after take-off.

One method of evaluating how much concern a larger airport has about noise is to measure the distance between the runways and the position and angle of take-off which they lead to in relation to the nearest settlements. Newer airports may have more space, which helps noise reduction, but they use up more land in achieving this. The airport authorities may also be judged on their voluntary efforts to reduce noise. They may impose restrictions on night flying. They may provide an extensive sound protection programme for local residents, installing double glazing and other forms of sound proofing. They may also carry out a regular noise monitoring procedure.

Air pollution has always been a concern in the vicinity of airports, with widespread beliefs that exhaust emissions and discharged fuel were a serious problem. Kerosene, used to fuel most aircraft, can be burned without much residue but some pollutants will still make their way into the atmosphere. It is not always easy ,however, to establish where the main responsibility for air pollution lies, since road traffic, industry and private households may all disperse pollutants into the atmosphere in the vicinity of airports. Modern aircraft use less fuel than their predecessors, largely as a result of better design and reduced weight. Emergency landings can, however, require fuel to be dumped so that a safe landing weight can be achieved. This is usually done 5000 feet above the ground which means that the speed of the aircraft causes the fuel to disperse into tiny droplets which eventually evaporate.

The extent of air pollution in the vicinity of airports is, not surprisingly, governed by the amount of traffic. Pilots arriving at busier airports may find there is a queue waiting to land. Aeroplanes fly in holding patterns, circling the airport until there is a suitable landing opportunity. The rate of air pollution created at individual airports can be established by setting up monitoring stations to measure the concentration of pollutants such as sulphur dioxide, carbon monoxide, nitrogen oxides, hydrocarbons and dust.

The siting of a new airport has implications for the existing environment. The planners

The siting of an airport has several implications for the environment.

will wish to have approaches which are thinly populated, both to reduce the risk to the population and to limit the nuisance to them during and after construction. This usually means a countryside location with the accompanying problems of tree felling, drainage and wildlife disturbance. Larger airports will also demand the construction of a good transport network, as well as the means of supplying efficient power and sewage systems.

Airports are usually built on flat, low-lying land and this in turn usually means that there is some natural flow of groundwater present. Without care construction can interfere with this, lowering the water table and affecting land and wildlife in the surrounding areas. The foundations for airport runways need to be frost-proof and so the land used is drained so that the water cannot rise too close to the surface. Some newly constructed airports have systems of channelling water through dykes to reduce the impact on the surrounding water levels. Modern instruments can measure accurately both groundwater levels and chemical purity.

Measuring the quality of water in the surrounding areas is important since airports use a number of chemicals which harm the natural environment. In winter runways have to be kept free of ice and snow to make landings safe. Additionally the wings and fuselage of a departing aeroplane also have to have any ice removed. De-icing agents, using glycol, are employed. An airport sensitive to the environment will have installed systems preventing any contaminated meltwater being left in the ground. One modern method of doing this is to use bacteria to convert the glycol into water and carbon dioxide.

An airport generates a large amount of rubbish which can impose considerable strain on local refuse services. Though the local authority or private refuse collection company will have responsibility for removing the waste, the policy of the airport managers may indicate the level of their concern about the environment. For example, they may take responsibility for reducing its volume or recycling materials made of glass, paper or metal. Many of the airport operations which generate waste, such as catering, are likely to be franchised out to private companies so that some airport authorities might argue that the problem was often outside their control.

Runways, aircraft, airport buildings, perimeter fences and access roads cannot be said to improve the appearance of many environments. An airport can perhaps best be judged in this respect by the extent to which the developers have tried to limit the damage. Sometimes developers enter into an agreement to compensate for the loss of land use by creating landscape conservation areas around the perimeters. This can combine the creation of a nature reserve with an improvement in the visual appearance of the site. Its drawback is the cost and the fact that it may consume additional land. The use of low level buildings and the planting of trees and shrubs are indications that some consideration has been given to the airport's visual impact on the environment.

Some forms of wildlife, particularly larger birds which can be a risk to aircraft, are unwelcome at airports. Various visual and aural devices may be used to scare them off. Modern airports also plant vegetation such as forage grass which is not attractive either to larger birds or to ground insects which might attract feeding birds.

One aspect of an airport's impact on the environment which is often overlooked is their huge consumption of energy. Heating, lighting and refrigeration all require a power supply. Like all major energy users, the environmental impact can be reduced by economic working practices, such as installing good insulation and ensuring that heat and light systems are efficient enough not to provide excess.

Your tasks

1 Discuss the following questions arising from statements made in the text:

a) On the basis of what facilities and services might a passenger assess the quality of an airport?
What factors would be used by the local community to judge both the airport's impact and its performance ?

b) Whose responsibility do you think it should be to assess the likely environmental impact of a new airport, particularly in an economically poor country?
Who do you think should pay for any measures proposed to protect the environment around a new airport ?

c) Identify the most common noises which annoy you. How many of these could be described as 'noise pollution'?

Can you come up with a definition of 'noise pollution' which you think might enable legal action to be taken against anyone found to be contributing to it ?

d) List the options available to an airport which decides that its monitoring stations are revealing an unacceptable level of air pollution.
Which of these options do you think are practical courses of action and what consequences might they have, apart from attempting to reduce the air pollution?

e) Suggest ways in which a farmer whose land abuts a new airport can judge its impact on his land and livestock.

f) What reasons can you provide for supporting or opposing the view that it is possible to 'compensate' for the loss of wildlife habitat?

2 Write a letter from a resident living in close proximity to an airport to whichever authority manages it.

The content of the letter should assess what the resident believes has been the impact of the airport on him/herself and on the community in which they live.

8.5 Evaluating the work of a museum – performance targets

Develops knowledge and understanding of the following element:
3   Evaluate the performance of a facility

Supports the development of the following core skills:
Application of number level 3: Interpret and present mathematical data (Task 1)
Communication level 3: Read and respond to written material and images, Application of number level 3: Interpret and present mathematical data (Task 2)

Measuring the performance of a leisure or tourism facility is much easier if there are specific targets to measure it against. These targets can relate to things which are easily quantifiable, such as the number of visitors or the average sales per visitor at retail outlets. In the case of a museum they are likely to include the design and opening of specific exhibitions. The refurbishment of buildings and the acquisition of new exhibits are likely to be included among short term objectives. Staffing levels and training and the overall income generated by the museum may be included in annual targets.

The Museum of London sets out its immediate targets in its Forward Plan which is published each year, reviewing the previous year's performance and relating it to plans for the five years ahead. The Plan has first to take account of the broad aims of the Museum. The main purposes of the Museum are to establish and care for collections, to exhibit them to the public, to make them available for research and to promote an understanding and appreciation of the history and culture of the city. The Forward Plan divides the achievement of the Museum into five different areas: the collections, public programmes, staff, buildings and expenditure and income.

A number of targets were set in the 1991–6 Plan for the collections. These included computerising the central inventory of items held by the Museum, moving a number of collections of items to different sites and reviewing policies and procedures relating to the acquisition and disposal of items. Much of this work was completed during 1991-2 and analysis showed that the main reason for some tasks remaining undone was due to the fact that not all curatorial posts were filled during the year and that a number of those who were appointed were only employed on a temporary basis. During the year other areas were identified as being in need of work, in particular an upgrading of the care of collections and a review of the research policy operated by the Museum. The extent of any task involving an overall review of the various collections held by the Museum is more evident when it is remembered that these collections have been estimated to contain over a million items.

A research programme, giving a monthly review of visitor profiles and reactions, was conducted during 1991. Apart from its marketing value, the programme helped in the planning of new displays and in the writing of accompanying captions and text. Evaluat-

The Museum of London

ing each permanent and temporary display plays an important part in the development of the Museum's public programmes. To fulfil the Museum's function of providing an educational experience, displays have to appeal to a wide age range and to take account of intellectual and linguistic differences among the visitors. Evaluation of a museum's public programmes could lead to a number of potential improvements. For example it might suggest that existing tours could be extended, or that publications should be updated, or that new exhibitions are required to cover previously neglected themes or periods. Many museums have responded to the National Curriculum by developing programmes aimed specifically at schools.

Achieving performance targets depends to some extent on maintaining satisfactory staffing levels. Changes in funding arrangements and the levels of supporting grants do not always coincide with the long-term plans of museums. Job specifications for individual employees are helpful in assessing their work load and deciding whether they are being used in the most effective way. This kind of review should also indicate the most urgent training needs.

Buildings and their condition are vital to any museum's continuing development. In 1991 The Museum of London planned to improve access to its stored collections and to the main Museum building. Annual budgets have to allow for the ageing process of the main buildings, which gradually increases the cost of remedial maintenance. A major project to extend the Museum's entrance area has been prepared and planning consents gained. Some environmental issues, such as the condition of buildings and developments in the area surrounding the Museum, may prove factors in the Museum's performance, even though they may be beyond the control of its managers.

The financial performance of a museum will set its earned income against its fixed overheads and operating costs. Earned income is estimated at the beginning of the year and will include money generated by admission charges, payments received from customers and clients, money recovered from VAT payments, and interest paid on investments. Fixed overheads will include money needed to finance and support the museum's premises, while operating costs cover such things as staff costs, transport, and supplies and services.

Each year's figures are generally accompanied by a commentary explaining where savings have been made or additional expenses incurred. For example if visitor numbers are higher than predicted, income will be correspondingly greater. If staff are made redundant, wages may be saved but redundancy agreements may prove a much greater drain on resources within a single financial year. Variations in interest rates will affect the financial performance of any museum which has borrowed money in the past for redevelopment and still has outstanding debts. The unpredictability of this factor makes budgeting for the coming year particularly difficult.

Financial targets for specific projects are easier to set. For example the Museum of London set a specific target in 1991–2 for the income it hoped to secure from hiring space to organisations for functions and conferences. The advantage of sponsorship is often that a fixed sum is agreed which helps budgeting and planning. However, even that can be affected by changes in the rate of inflation during the year, leading to costs which may be higher or, less frequently, lower than expected.

Your tasks

The Easthampton Museum has permanent exhibitions illustrating life in the town from the Middle Ages to the end of the Second World War. It also houses a collection of water colours by Sir Piers Bective, a native of the town, and an exhibition of the furniture made by a local chair manufacturing firm, the Seaton Downing Company, between its establishment in 1880 and its closure in 1976.

The Museum's Redevelopment Policy aims gradually to modernise its collections and to broaden the range of services it offers to the local community. A Museum Improvement Fund was established in 1985, largely through legacies from the Bective and Downing families, and its investments yield a modest but regular income.

1 What changes are evident in the Museum's performance from Tables 1 and 2 below?

Table 1 Admissions to Easthampton Museum (1988–91)

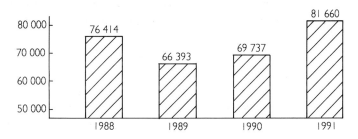

Table 2 Annual average sales per visitor (1988–91)

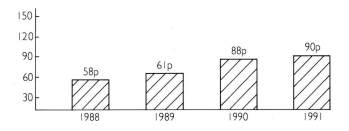

List the possible reasons which account for these changes.

2 Table 3 is an extract from a more extensive list of performance indicators for 1991. Assuming that this extract is typical of the rest of the document, what conclusions could you draw about the performance of the facility over the year?

Table 3   Performance indicators 1991: Easthampton Museum

	Target	Action area	Performance indicator	Analysis
A	To produce a design for a 'Roman Easthampton' gallery	1 Appoint and approve designer 2 Submit scheme to Museum Improvement Fund Council	1 Compliance with Museum Redevelopment policy	Scheme delayed due to deferral of funds by MIFC into next financial year
B	Re-sign Bective watercolour exhibition	1 Design graphic text 2 Edit 3 Approve design and budget	1 Measure against exhibition management document 2 Measure against pre-set budget	Running to schedule
C	Acquire further furniture exhibits	1 Compile potential list 2 Survey space 3 Set/approve budget 4 Acquire	1 Measure against visitor survey comment 2 Measure against pre-set budget	1 Still to be evaluated 2 £3450 against pre-set budget of £3000
D	Refurbish/improve 'study area'	1 Install new shelving 2 Replace old prints 3 Install photocopier	Measure against Museum Redevelopment Policy	Ran to schedule

8.6 Evaluating the financial performance of a guest house

Develops knowledge and understanding of the following element:

3   Evaluate the performance of a facility

Supports the development of the following core skills:

Application of number level 3: Represent and tackle problems, Interpret and present mathematical data (Task 1)

Application of number level 3: Interpret and present mathematical data (Task 2)

Communication level 3: Read and respond to written material and images (Task 3)

'Stumbleside' is a small guest house in the Lake District. Established in their stone-built former family home by Mr and Mrs Reg Guest in the 1930s, it is now run by their son, Phil, and his wife, Sue.

Running a small business like this is not just a matter of sitting and waiting for people to arrive in the summer holidays. There are all year round costs involved in running a guest house and the owners aim must be to keep it as full as possible for as long as possible. The Lake District attracts people during all holidays, including Easter, Whit, Christmas and school half terms. It is also a popular destination with people looking for weekend or mid-week short breaks.

In previous years Stumbleside has achieved an occupancy rate of approximately 60 per cent. As a business it does currently make a net profit, even when the owners draw personal wages of £5000. This sum is agreed with the Inland Revenue as being a reasonable wage to draw, being roughly what it would cost to employ someone else to do the work involved. The owners will have to pay some tax on any profit they make.

Cashflow figures play an important role in running any business. Even in a profitable business it may prove impossible to pay debts at particular times of year if the movement of cash through the business is not properly managed. If all creditors decide to call in the money owed to them at the same time a company can become insolvent, despite the expectation that it would have made a profit over the whole year. For many businesses this means they have to borrow money and repay it when their revenue is at its peak. Cashflow calculations enable a business to predict the flow of money over time and to plan strategies to cope with periods showing a deficit.

The owners of Stumbleside have a number of possible ways of improving cash flow. They can reinvest their profits into the business. They could seek to defer or spread their payments more evenly. The latter can be done by using budget bank accounts to pay some bills in instalments. They could seek higher deposits or earlier payments from their customers or tighten up on their procedures for extracting some sort of compensatory payment from customers who make late cancellations.

Your tasks

Study the business summary and the cashflow summary on the following pages and then answer the questions which follow on page 88.

Stumbleside Guest House: summary of current business

1. Location The Lake District

2. Season February–December plus Christmas/New Year period. Closed 7 January–14 February approx.

3. Rooms 5 x double occupancy, 2 x single occupancy, 1 x family occupancy (four maximum including two children up to 16 years of age)

4. Rates per night (Bed & breakfast)

	Adults (£)	Children (one free if sharing) (%)	Single supplement (£)
Feb–Mar (46 nights)	12	50	1
April–May (61 nights)	14	50	1
June–Sept (122 nights)	15	50	2

Continued overleaf

Stumbleside Guest House: Summary of current business continued

Oct–Nov (61 nights)	12	50	I
I Dec–21 Dec (21 nights)	11	50	nil
21 Dec–7 Jan (18 nights)	15	50	2

The 47-week opening period (329 nights) aims at 60 per cent occupancy at adult rates, disregarding child reductions and room supplements. In other words 14 adult beds per night represents 100 per cent occupancy.

5. Maximum possible revenue

$46 \times £12 \times 14 = £7728$
$61 \times £14 \times 14 = £11\ 956$
$122 \times £15 \times 14 = £25\ 620$
$61 \times £12 \times 14 = £10\ 248$
$21 \times £11 \times 14 = £3234$
$18 \times £15 \times 14 = £3780$

Total $= £62\ 566$

6. Anticipated revenue

$60\% \times £62\ 566 = £37\ 500$

7. Actual revenue

Sales	B & B room occupancy	36 784			
	Packed lunches	494			
		37 278			37 278
Less:					
Cost of sales	Bedding	941			
	Food ingredients/grocery	2100			
		3041			
				3041	
	Overheads				
	Mortgage	4980			
	Light/heat/water	948			
	Rates (Unified Business)	3500			
	Repairs and maintenance	2000			
	Drawings (owners' salaries)	5000			
	Other salaries/wages	4300			
	Insurance	752			
	Telephone	842			
	Stationery	759			
	Advertising	650			
	Postages	700			
	Sundry items	451			
		24 882			
			24 882		
			27 923		27 923
	Net profit				9355

Stumbleside Guest House: Actual cashflow for trading year February 1992–January 1993

Item	F	M	A	M	J	J	A	S	O	N	D	J	Notes
Revenue													
B&B	1274	3362	3196	3958	3132	3684	4188	4368	4184	1229	3141	1068	(36784)
Other	24	42	38	45	44	52	60	64	52	28	35	10	(494) Fewer lunches in bad weather
Total income	1298	3404	3234	4003	3176	3736	4248	4432	4236	1257	3176	1078	(37278)
Costs													
Food	84	165	142	178	212	172	424[1]	211	192	68	102	150	(2100) [1]Bulk purchase
Bedding	424	–	–	–	317	–	–	200	–	–	–	–	(941)
Mortgage	415	415	415	415	415	415	415	415	415	415	415	415	(4980)
Light/heat/water	82	64	74	80	78	82	68	84	94	90	88	64	(948) Varies with demands for hot water, heat, etc.
Rates (Unified business)	–	–	1750	–	–	–	–	1750	–	–	–	–	(3500) Twice p.a.
Repairs/maintenance	984[2]	–	–	250	42	150	40	–	92	400[3]	42	42	(2000) [2]Decoration while closed [3]Burst pipe
Drawings	–	1250	–	–	1250	1250	–	1250	–	–	1250	–	(5000) Quarterly for proprietor
Salaries/wages	100	120	200	400	550	560	600	610	421	329	300	110	(4300) Spouse plus casual staff employed
Insurance	–	548[4]	–	–	–	204[5]	–	–	–	–	–	–	(752) 2 × Annual premiums; [4]Public liability; [5]Buildings
Telephone	226	–	–	236	–	–	192	–	–	188	–	–	(842) Quarterly
Stationery	32	30	40	28	22	25	28	20	18	–	410	106	(759)
Advertising	254	–	–	–	–	–	–	–	–	–	–	396	(650) Seasonal items to attract customers
Postage	174	82	50	48	56	12	14	40	32	30	34	128	(700)
Sundries	10	18	–	121	39	80	74	22	37	0	0	32	(451)
Total costs	2785	2692	2671	1756	2981	1700	1855	4602	1301	1529	2608	1443	(27 923)
Surplus/deficit	–1487	+712	+563	+2247	+195	+2036	+2393	–170	+2935	–272	+568	–365	
Funds available at:													
a) the start of month	2000	513	1225	1788	4035	4230	6266	8659	8489	11 424	11 152	11 720	(including £20000 b/f Feb 92)
b) the end of month	513	1225	1788	4035	4230	6266	8659	8489	11 424	11 152	11 72 0	11 355	

Assignments in Leisure and Tourism

1 a) Identify which expenses are unavoidable in the early months of the calendar year, even though income is low, and explain why this is so.

b) Which was the guest house's best month for sales and why did it not make a profit in that month?

c) What would happen to September's deficit figures if occupancy was increased by 10 per cent, taking into account that additional food, costing £40, would have to be bought in?

d) Do you see any opportunity for other sales to boost total income, in addition to packed lunches?

e) What reasons can you suggest for the fact that May revenue exceeds that of June, even though room rates charged in June are higher?

f) What factors should the owners take into account in deciding the relative room rates fixed for May and June?

g) What arguments can you think of for and against the owners keeping the guest house open in November and early December?

h) Why might it be a good idea for the owners to use budget bank accounts as a means of settling some of their expenditure?

i) If the Guests were attempting to buy the hotel now, as opposed to fifteen years ago when they bought it from the senior Guests, they would need a larger mortgage, approximately doubling their monthly repayments. Indicate the consequences of this for the monthly profitability of the business.

j) Can you think of ways in which the Guests might boost occupancy or provide added value which would enable them to increase prices?

k) The average price of an 8-bedroomed house in the Lake District similar to Stumbleside is £60 000. Explain why you would or would not be willing to pay £80 000 for the 'Stumbleside' guest house business.

2 Read the article below taken from 'The Lake District Echo' published on 7 February 1993:

Hotels and guesthouses suffered in 1992

'One of the Lake District's major employment sectors is suffering badly in the present economic climate.

A good May last year, with guesthouses in particular about 60 per cent full, was followed by a poor June with less than 50 per cent average bed occupancy.

The only boom month was September with popular addresses recording up to 90% figures in the excellent Indian summer which attracted older visitors to The Lakes after the end of the school holidays. This helped offset the disastrously wet June, July and August, when often three beds in four went unsold each night and a 50 per cent occupancy rate was regarded as a success.

October and November were better than some expected with up to 55% figures in some businesses, but the very miserable Christmas weather left our area almost empty. "You were doing better than many if 10 per cent of beds went daily," said Mo Smart on behalf of the local hospitality association.

Now there is a threat hanging over the new season. Guests are preferring establishments offering evening meals. "Owners will have to respond even though the requirement to provide food around 7–8 p.m. often hardly covers the costs,"said a representative of the Regional Tourist Board.'

Use the article and the data you have about Stumbleside to evaluate the performance of the business over the year.

8.7 Evaluating the business performance of a leisure park

Develops knowledge and understanding of the following element:

3   Evaluate the performance of a facility

Supports the development of the following core skills:

Communication level 3: Take part in discussions, Application of number level 3;
    Represent and tackle problems, Interpret and present mathematical data (Task 1)
Communication level 3: Take part in discussions, Application of number level 3;
    Interpret and present mathematical data (Task 2)

Leisure parks, like most other businesses, exist to make a profit. As a result the measurement of their success must include the setting of financial targets which are likely to be divided into two main categories: the return on the capital invested, and the trading margin.

Gardens at Alton Towers

A successful leisure park will certainly require investment. The cost of purchasing a new ride, for example, can be in excess of £10 million. If the park is starting from scratch, as in the case of EuroDisney, the amount of new investment will be higher than that needed in an established park. Funds will be needed for construction, legal and architects' fees, landscaping, and salaries before any income has been generated. An older park is likely to have a broader capital base. This means more of the money it needs to operate, including investment in new development, is likely to come from its own assets which have been derived from previous years' profits or from its own successful investments.

Pearson plc, the owners of Alton Towers, invested some £60 million in the Park in 1990. If they had put that sum into a building society in that year, they might have received 15 per cent interest as a return on their investment. Investing the money in a leisure park is regarded as carrying a higher risk and so investors require a higher return, in this case possibly in excess of 25 per cent. In other words Pearsons might have set a financial objective for Alton Towers for 1990, aiming for a return of £15 million.

Regardless of the level of investment, a leisure park will measure its trading profitability. This is essentially a matter of subtracting costs from sales. The trading margin must be sufficient to generate a return on the capital investment. In other words, as for any other business, it is not enough for a leisure park company simply to make a trading profit.

At Alton Towers management accounts are published annually, though the data for these is internally circulated on a quarterly basis. The accounts take the form of a profit and loss account, which gives a financial measure of performance over a period of time. Such accounts can be accompanied by a commentary offering views about trends identified within them, for example high costs in a particular area might be the result of possible over-staffing.

Alton Towers

The advantage of quarterly reviews of figures is that they avoid the difficulty of judging on a month by month basis, where fluctuations can be misleading. Quarterly figures also enable comparisons to be made between years on a seasonal basis. If the figures revealed that business performance was not as good as had been expected, a number of immediate responses might be possible. It might be possible to reduce overheads in some way. Discount offers or special deals might be used to try and attract more visitors. It might be possible to offer added value without a very high investment, for example by offering a free guide book or by offering free admission to a child accompanied by a paying adult.

The Alton Towers accounts will include forecasts of future income, derived from admission charges and from secondary sales through food and retail outlets. Income is dependent on the volume of visitors and their individual spend. Since all leisure parks have a finite capacity, the upper limits of income are fixed as long as the admission price remains the same. Leisure park customers are unlikely to respond positively to price increases unless they feel some additional value has been provided. This means that profit growth is dependent on capital investment, since that is the best way of improving the product and thus allowing acceptable price increases and a rise in income.

Your tasks

The two pie charts below represent the percentage of total expenditure in a medium-sized leisure park devoted to different categories in the years 1991 and 1992.

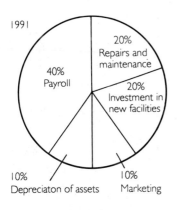

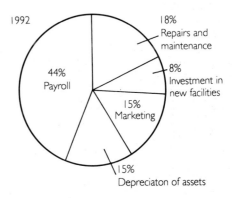

I Discuss what evidence you can see to suggest that the following statements are either probably true, possibly true, unlikely, or impossible to determine:

   a) More staff were employed in 1991 than 1992.

   b) An evaluation of 1990's business performance suggested some added value was needed.

   c) Television advertising was first tried in 1992.

   d) Older equipment has proved more costly to maintain over this two-year period.

   e) Investing in new facilities has long term financial implications.

2 The leisure park management consider that 1992 was a success and they predict that the number of visitors will continue to increase in 1993.

Assuming that this proves to be the case, discuss the various possible implications of the two following expenditure forecasts for 1993.

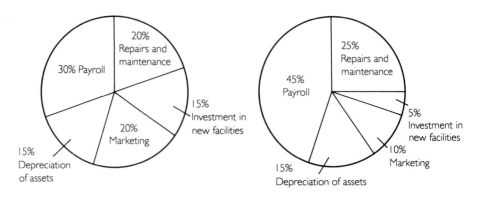